GUILD OF THE
HEARERS
WATCHERS
SPEAKERS
SENSERS
PROPHETS

ESSENTIAL HANDBOOKS
FOR CHRISTIANS

VOL.
I

THE
FOUNDATIONS
OF THE PROPHETIC

VOL.

I

ANDREW BILLINGS

WITH A FOREWORD BY: DR. ROBB THOMPSON

CONTENTS

FOREWORD

The old prophet would wander into town and send shivers down the spines of all those who lived in that particular place. For when he came to town, the people there wanted to know if the word that was on his lips was a positive word, or whether it was a word speaking of the demise of the people who were now standing before him. The Old Testament is filled with such scenarios.

The Bible tells of the time God spoke to Samuel as a little boy, who grew up and let none of his words fall to the ground. God spoke by Elijah, Jeremiah, or Isaiah; He spoke by the mouths of Elisha, Ezekiel, and Daniel. There were not only words that came from the mouths of the prophets that changed the course of history, but there were others who lived their lives prophetically, speaking of and declaring God's goodness. These prophetic people declared God's faithfulness and integrity, no matter the circumstances they faced.

The book of Hebrews speaks of those who lived a prophetic life, those who lived a life of faith:

> By faith these people overthrew kingdoms, ruled with justice, and received what God had promised them. They shut the mouths of lions, quenched the flames of fire, and escaped death by the edge of the sword. Their weakness was turned to strength. They became strong in battle and put whole armies to flight. Women received their loved ones back again from death.
>
> But others were tortured, refusing to turn from God in order to be set free. They placed their hope in a better life

after the resurrection. Some were jeered at and their backs were cut open with whips. Others were chained in prisons. Some died by stoning, some were sawed in half, and others were killed with the sword. Some went about wearing skins of sheep and goats, destitute and oppressed and mistreated. They were too good for this world, wandering over deserts and mountains, hiding in caves and holes in the ground.

All these people earned a good reputation because of their faith, yet none of them received all that God had promised (Hebrews 11:33–39 NLT).

The Old Testament prophet's vision was greatly expanded as he approached the New Testament. The Old Testament prophet is now flanked with the aid of the New Testament believer who prophesies, speaks in tongues, interprets those tongues, and who receives a word of wisdom or knowledge. What was thought unusual in the Old Testament has now become more normative in the New Testament, as all God's people have received of his Spirit.

What you will discover in the Guild of the Prophets is much more than a history lesson of the prophetic. Rather, it is an instruction manual on how to live your life as a prophet, or how to live your life as a prophetic person. This is only the first out of seven books in this series. I would encourage you to get them, read them, and learn from them. I know that I have learned much just from this first volume alone.

—Dr. Robb Thompson

INTRODUCTION

I want to personally welcome you to the start of this incredible journey through your schooling as a prophet as you begin this series called The Guild of the Prophets. This book is designed to be read first in the series. It will serve as a stand-alone resource, but also as an introduction to the realm of the prophetic and the office of the prophet, which will be covered in more detail throughout the rest of the series. There are many concepts presented here that are only a gateway to the depth contained in the following six books.

The Guild of the Prophets is designed to be both informative and equipping, creating a written form of the school of the prophets, bringing forth character, moral benchmarks, and standards to this area that is the most unusual of all the gifts and operations of the Spirit. It is my hope that this book will also bring a level of understanding to the often most misunderstood of all the gifts—prophecy and prophets.

This whole series is designed to walk a young prophet through his or her development into levels of maturity in which he or she can walk in integrity and be a blessing to the church. Not only that, but it is my hope that the prophet would mature and be a blessing to the wider context of his or her community into which God places him or her. Not only is this series written for young prophets, but it is also written for those who may not be gifted or geared that way. It is important that we understand our various positions and roles in the body of Christ. In order to do that, we need to go to the beginning and examine the foundations of this amazing aspect of the kingdom of God.

The Guild of the Prophets started as a personal quest back in 2009 to examine the roles and office of the prophetic, and to look at why it sometimes succeeds and why it sometimes fails. Now with more than a hundred chapters spread out over seven books, this gives the reader the opportunity to delve into and get a glimpse at just how far-reaching the facets are of this aspect of God. Even then, this book does not fully define this part of God's nature; it is merely an introduction to His eternal and limitless character. I pray that God would give you the Spirit of wisdom and understanding as you read this book. (Ephesians 1:17)

—Andrew Billings

CHAPTER 1

WHAT IS THE PROPHETIC?

Since before time ever began to tick, God was already speaking and declaring His will and His purposes throughout the earth. His creative power knows no limits, and it is something we all should be aware of in our personal walks with Him. The realm of the prophetic is often seen as some mystical experience or office, but it's really quite simple when we stop to think about it. The truth is that everything in God is quite simple if we truly come to the kingdom with childlike hearts.

The prophetic realm is simply an avenue God uses to bring His world—His messages, words, and will—into our world. He oftentimes uses people to do this, while at other times He allows the signs to speak for themselves. Oftentimes these messages can come directly from God to a specific individual, while at other times God places a strong message or unction in someone and they declare certain thoughts to the person for whom it's intended.

To most people, there is a focused aspect to the realm of prophecy, accurately describing or predicting what will happen in the future. But the truth is that it's so much more than this. The prophetic is really the expressed reflection of God's heart, His love, and His will being communicated to humankind through many different ways. It can involve creative acts, guidance, forewarnings, or even corrections and announcements from the Lord, along with understanding of present moments and revelations from the past.

God-given prophecy offers understanding, insight, promise, and hope not only for future events, but also for present and past events too. The gift of prophecy reveals God's heart and His intentions over the purposes of individuals, groups, and nations of the world, and their respective destinies as planned by Father God from before the foundation of the earth. The prophetic is like a platform from which God is able to convey His heart, plans, judgments, and guidance to the entire planet through various ways and expressions.

While many people believe that the prophetic is only for the saved—those who are Christians—they are missing out on the value of this precious gift. Do you remember how, in the time of Joseph, Pharaoh had dreams that came from God in which he was forewarned about the famine that was to come in the land? Pharaoh was a pagan king, not a part of God's redeemed people, and yet God spoke to him through dreams in the night. Yes, Joseph had to interpret them, but God still gave them to a man who didn't follow Him. The same can be seen in Daniel's life while he was serving as an advisor and interpreter of dreams to four different ungodly kings. God speaks and prophetically reveals His heart to *all* people, not just His sons and daughters.

A GIFT GIVEN BY GOD

In our discussion of the prophetic, it is important to understand that the act or ability of describing future events, operating as an oracle or mouthpiece of the divine, revealing a truth that may be unknown to others, or having prophetic abilities, is not a self-generated talent. Rather, it is a gift from God. The gift can become so intertwined with the prophet's persona that at times there is a misconception that he or she is somehow the producer of the gift. But this is an error. It is only God who gives these gifts to individuals, and, since they are gifts, that means we are only stewards of what we did not earn. And so I caution everyone at this point: never make the mistake that you are the source of your anointing or your gift. It is given to you by God alone.

Paul lists the nine gifts of the Spirit in 1 Corinthians 12:4–11. Before we get too far into our discussion, it would be important to briefly look at this passage. It is important to note that all of these gifts come from the same Spirit, which means they are given by God, and that God is the one who gives them to individuals as He desires.

There are diversities of gifts, but the same Spirit. There are differences of ministries, but the same Lord. And there are diversities of activities, but it is the same God who works all in all. But the manifestation of the Spirit is given to each one for the profit of all: for to one is given the word of wisdom through the Spirit, to another the word of knowledge through the same Spirit, to another faith by the same Spirit, to another gifts of healings by the same Spirit, to another the working of miracles, to another prophecy, to another discerning of spirits, to another different kinds of tongues, to another the interpretation of tongues. But one and the same Spirit works all these things, distributing to each one individually as He wills.

Three of these gifts are prophetic in nature. They are prophecy, the word of knowledge, and the word of wisdom. The prophetic *gift* is bestowed on a person by the Spirit of God, and it is simply that—a gift. There is nothing that a person can do to earn this gift—it is given only by God, which means that the entire body of Christ can operate in and function in this gift from time to time since we all have His Spirit.

HEARING GOD'S VOICE

I want to be clear from the outset that functioning in these gifts does not make an individual a prophet in the same way driving a car does not make you a car. Yes, you are a driver, but you're not a car. In much the same way, all of God's children can prophesy, but not all are called to be prophets—not all are called to fulfill the office of a prophet.

The prophetic gift is given for the whole body of Christ to operate in, but the office of the prophet is reserved only for those whom

God calls. Think about it like this: Not everyone is called to be an evangelist, but every son or daughter of God is called to operate in sharing the gospel with unbelievers—we are all called to evangelize people with whom we come into contact. The same is true when it comes to the office of the prophet. Just as an evangelist is an office some are called to fulfill, so the office of the prophet is only for those whom God calls, but all believers are called to operate in the prophetic gifts.

In John 10:26–27, Jesus talked to His disciples about those who are able to hear His voice and those who are not able to hear it. He clearly says that there is a group of people who do not believe Him because they are not His "sheep," they are not His people, and there is a group of people who do believe Him. Then He says about those who do believe in Him, "My sheep hear My voice, and I know them, and they follow Me" (John 10:27).

There can be times or seasons in our walk with God when the voice of God seems scarce. When a newly saved child of God enters his or her walk with God, there can also be a learning curve when first learning to hear His voice. But the frequency of hearing Jesus's voice is not what Jesus is pointing out here. He is pointing out the important point that we, as His sons and daughters, are able to hear and recognize His voice because we are His sheep.

Jesus refers to all of us—those of us whose hearts have been born again by saving faith in the death and resurrection of Jesus— metaphorically as sheep who know the voice of their master. That means all of us can at times interact with the prophetic realm and hear God's voice or perceive what is on His heart, but that does not qualify us as prophets.

So these three prophetic gifts—prophecy, the word of knowledge, and the word of wisdom—make up a third of the gifts of the Spirit listed by Paul in 1 Corinthians 12. They are given to us to establish God's kingdom here on earth. As a prophet or a prophetic person, it's important that we pay attention to the traits of these gifts in our pursuit of God. Let's take a close look at the gift of prophecy and the office of the prophet.

THE PROPHETIC IS ROOTED AND GROUNDED IN LOVE

Again, at the outset I think it is important to note that the prophetic realm is rooted and grounded in love. Paul wrote, "Watch, stand fast in the faith, be brave, be strong. Let all you do be done with love" (1 Corinthians 16:13–14). The idea presented in this verse is fundamentally important when it comes to moving in the prophetic or holding the office of a prophet. Everything that God says comes from a place and heart of love. You must grasp this concept, otherwise nothing else you read in this series will be interpreted correctly, and you may misunderstand God in the area of your life and ministry.

Both the gentle and the strong statements and actions God has made from the beginning are all grounded in and motivated by love. After all, isn't God the embodiment of love? In order to correctly represent Him, we need to focus on what love actually looks like and filter all we say and all we do through a heart and expression of love.

Contrary to popular opinion, love is not just warm and cuddly, as some have painted it. Yes, it is warm and cuddly at times, but love is also nurturing, it is life-giving. Love is encouraging and it believes the best; love desires restoration and justice. Loves sees God-given destiny in someone's life and agrees with it and thus calls it out.

Most of us know that love is gentle and kind, but it also can be strong and direct, which at times can be easily misunderstood. There is such a thing as "tough love." An example of this is easily seen in Hebrews 12:6–12, as it explains that the chastening and correction of the Lord is applied to those He loves. Love does not just empower a person to feel good about his or her dysfunctional situation, but it will confront in such a way that freedom is available for that particular individual.

Many people misunderstand love in our time. People often believe that "love covers over a matter," which means that we are to cover other people's sins and shortcomings. This is true to a point. However, to only believe that love covers sins shows an imbalance of understanding and a level of immaturity in this facet of God's nature. Love also rejoices in the truth. It is not afraid of the truth and loving confrontation. God confronts us and even rebukes and scourges us in order to refine us and fashion us to be free from sin and ready for His grand design that He has dreamed over us (Hebrews 12:6–12).

Simply overlooking certain issues is a lack of love and could even be unloving at times. In other words, it would be unloving to see someone who is steps away from walking over a cliff and fail to confront them about the danger ahead all in the name of believing the best and covering over the fact that they cannot see what is ahead of them. Love is bold enough to speak what is needed in the moment through a right heart for the person's well-being and destiny.

This type of tough love can be seen in Matthew 16. Peter was attempting to talk Jesus out of going to the cross and dying, and Jesus, in a seemingly stern moment, responded to Peter's comment by telling Satan to get behind Him, because he was an offense to God. Jesus needed to address the spiritual atmosphere that was pressuring Him not to go ahead with the Father's plans of the cross. Peter had come into agreement with the atmosphere and so Jesus needed to speak out against it. This needed to happen not just to rebuke Satan, but also for Peter's benefit so that he could realize the error of his thinking. And this was the most loving thing to do in that moment.

Tough love can also be seen when Jesus entered the temple and overturned the tables there. Leaders were taking advantage of the people in the gathering place that was meant exclusively for God's purpose, and instead they had set up shops to make money. They had taken a holy place and made it a market of trading. This displeased Jesus because He was in tune with the heart of the Father. So He made a whip and turned merchandise tables over. Jesus loved the Father so much, and He also loved the people so much, that in love He confronted their error, which had actually become an insult to God.

The reason for Jesus's outburst? I believe it was a drastic statement against a popular belief with the hopes of snapping people out of the spell that had taken away their reverence and fear of the Lord. This offered an opportunity to reconcile with the original design of interaction through God's model. Jesus said, "It is written, 'My house shall be called a house of prayer,' but you have made it a 'den of thieves'" (Matthew 21:13). That sounds harsh, right? Actually, it was love crying out for a return to intimacy with the Father.

It's important that in all of our loving, we love God first. And as a result of loving God first, we will then love people correctly.

And let's not forget about the time when Ananias and Sapphira lied to the Holy Spirit (Acts 5:1–11). They had conspired together and lied to Peter about a piece of property they sold and the amount they collected from that. Peter questioned them each separately and they both lied, holding to their conspired story, when there was actually no real reason to lie at all. Peter confronted them and told them that they had lied to the Holy Spirit, and as a result both Ananias and Sapphira dropped dead. It is interesting that after this happened, the church began to thrive and increase (Acts 5:12–16).

The reason I am using these three examples is because they are New Testament instances in which expressions of love took place under the New Covenant. If those instances happened today, in our time at the local church, a prophet may be labeled as harsh or unloving. Maybe our current culture has just reshaped what we want God to look like, and what love's definition is supposed to be. But we clearly see that love can express itself in ways that are opposite to what today's popular Christian culture describes it. We must find love Himself to understand this.

God's heart will always look to operate in redemptive love. We can see a beautiful example of the prophetic flowing through Jesus's ministry in the fact that He never pressured anyone; rather, He merely set options out and honored each person's personal sovereignty enough to let him or her choose what he or she wanted. Many times He said, "I set before you life and death, but I urge you to choose life." There's no condemnation or manipulation in that statement, just a message with a decision that needs to be made. The same heart is expressed from Jesus when He talked to the woman at the well, and when He told the rich young ruler that he had indeed kept all of the law, but there was more still to be done—he should go sell all he had and give it to the poor and then come follow Jesus.

Love does not just speak kind, positive statements. Love will confront and call out dysfunction in lives and communities in order to see positive changes realized. Love will correct and challenge. It will exhort people to live in a manner that is holy while not neglecting what God has said. There are moments when you will be required to confront with truth and be labeled as harsh, and that's okay. Always follow the Spirit of God when He asks you to speak in those moments. Many of the Old Testament prophets were rejected and even killed due to the fact that people rejected their message, and in doing so blamed the messenger. Love anyway.

PERCEIVING THE REDEMPTIVE HEART OF GOD

When I was younger, I needed time to learn this. Young prophets can be so full of zeal that they become frustrated when conveying the heart of God to people who don't always seem to receive it well. And so they can become harsh or angry in the way that they deliver the message. And you know what? Those prophecies hurt people, and then the young prophet is often stereotyped and shunned as a result. But just like a young teacher, pastor, or evangelist, the young prophet is learning and is going to make mistakes along the way. It's one thing to hear the voice of God, but if we don't receive or perceive the heart of God in that message, it may very well be conveyed wrong. We must not just be hearers and seers of prophetic messages, but we must learn to perceive the redemptive heart of God in each situation.

Jesus did not come to condemn the world, but to save it. And yet He was crucified because what He said was an offense to some of His hearers. He spoke truth and conveyed the heart of God in love, even though in some situations He called Pharisees vipers and foxes. And so we must learn the heart of God and filter what He is saying and doing through His heart, not our minds. In all your pursuit to grasp the prophetic gifts, may I encourage you to learn love. Echo Paul's prayer here as you engage on your prophetic journey:

> For this reason I bow my knees to the Father of our Lord
> Jesus Christ, from whom the whole family in heaven and
> earth is named, that He would grant you, according to the
> riches of His glory, to be strengthened with might through

His Spirit in the inner man, that Christ may dwell in your hearts through faith; that you, being rooted and grounded in love, may be able to comprehend with all the saints what is the width and length and depth and height—to know the love of Christ which passes knowledge; that you may be filled with all the fullness of God. (Ephesians 3:14–19)

Understanding the redemptive heart of God takes an immersion in the heart and love of the Father, a bold representation of what He is saying and doing, and a mantle and heart humbled before the Lord. This combination allows us to walk well in this area, to not only perceive but also steward what He shows us and asks us to do.

CHAPTER 2

THE PROPHET AND PROPHECY

The prophetic and the office of the prophet are often easily confused. The prophetic is like a world or avenue that at times overlaps and interrupts our present reality, through which God speaks and in which we interact. The gift of prophecy is a gift that any member of the body of Christ can tap into and function in from time to time, as the Spirit of God moves upon them. It is truly an amazing part of God's world that is made available for us.

The prophetic gift is an aspect of God's expressive nature that all believers can visit at times, whereas a prophet is a person who seems to be far more saturated in this facet and becomes an extension of God, or God's mouthpiece. Maybe a simple way to describe this would be to consider the prophetic realm like the Internet. Prophetic people access and look into it through a screen and interact with it at certain times when they use a device that is connected to Wi-Fi. So people see inward and glimpse information as needed.

A prophet, on the other hand, is more like the screen of a desktop computer that is connected to the Internet at all times. The device is connected more directly to the Internet, and objectively speaking, the screen looks back out at the world through the perspective and filters the information more directly. This is why prophets can seem odd and different in many situations—their perspectives and agendas can seem intense and even overboard at times. Prophetic people visit the prophetic realm on occasion, whereas prophets are more directly connected with a deeper or clearer grasp of what God is expressing. That is why many times throughout history prophets have been referred to as mystics, oracles, seers, wise men, or counselors and advisors.

THE DISTINCTION BETWEEN PROPHECY AND PROPHET

Prophecy is the delivery of a spiritual message into a specific situation. It can come in differing forms, but it always has the appearance of having an acute perception of a spiritual or natural reality of things to come, things happening, or things past. At times prophecy can be an utterance or physical outworking of something in obedience to the Spirit of God, which is not known by the person operating in the gift, but later he realizes the weighty relevance of what God was speaking into the atmosphere.

There are times when the person prophesying has a firm grasp on the concept of what he or she is delivering, and there are other times in which the person has no idea what the message means or its relevance to the recipient. When I have been prophesying, at times the message drops into my spirit and it is spoken out before I have had time to ponder or consider exactly what is being said. It seems as though God was possessing my being and speaking through me. Then there are other times where God just drops a statement or a picture into my heart, and I converse with Him about its meaning and relevance prior to opening my mouth. It is important to be led by God and grow in maturity and experience in this gift. There are also times when what God is revealing to you is not meant to be shared with those around you. This calls for a growth in wisdom to rightly steward these insights.

Then there is the office of a prophet. This person just doesn't operate in the gift of prophecy, but he or she has the hand of God on his or her life to be a mouthpiece for the Lord, like a pastor or teacher has an anointing specifically for the tasks set before them. God anoints prophets by His Spirit, not according to whether they are a man or woman, young or old, to speak His words wisely, at certain times to specific people.

The office of the prophet is part of the apostolic fivefold ministry that helps to guide, lead, steer, train, and equip the body of Christ. Paul wrote to the Ephesians to outline the purpose of this ministry:

> *And He Himself gave some to be apostles, some prophets, some evangelists, and some pastors and teachers, for the equipping of the saints for the work of ministry, for the edifying of the body of Christ, till we all come to the unity of the faith and of the knowledge of the Son of God, to a perfect man, to the measure of the stature of the fullness*

of Christ; that we should no longer be children, tossed to and fro and carried about with every wind of doctrine, by the trickery of men, in the cunning craftiness of deceitful plotting ... (Ephesians 4:11–14).

Possessing one of these five gifts does not make an individual a more important person or a more valuable person than anyone else, but it does give that person the opportunity to serve God faithfully by serving others in love. As they grow in maturity and serve in greater measures, then greater levels of honor are naturally due, but notoriety should never be a motivation to progress in this office.

I like to describe the office of a prophet as an avenue through which God reveals His plans, intentions, and dreams for the future of a person, a group of people, or a nation. That person reveals the voice of God regarding what is to come, which comes in a predictive sense, whether that is through blessing or judgment, or understanding or revelation. But the predictive voice of God can also come through guidance, wisdom, and cautionary warnings for present situations, directions and decisions.

Two examples come from the books of Daniel and Revelation. In these books we see God using a prophet as an oracle to speak and reveal things yet to come, both in quite cryptic descriptions. It is important to note that the prophetic is not always cryptic, however; sometimes it is plain and simple like when the prophet Samuel came to Saul when he had not obeyed the Lord by destroying all of the enemies, and had withheld a portion of what was to be offered to God. And sometimes it is like Jesus when He operated with a word of knowledge, telling the woman at the well about the five husbands she previously had as well as the current man in her life who was not her husband. From these two examples, we can see that the prophetic is definitely not a one-dimensional facet of God's nature.

When a man or woman is in tune with the Spirit of God, they are available to be used by God to deliver a message for Him. In the humblest description, a prophet or a person operating in the prophetic is simply a messenger for the Lord, an honorable servant of the King. Whether it is a gift being operated in or a person in the office of a prophet, the pure and accurate prophetic gift will always give direction or correction, hopes and dreams in which to agree with God, or to urge you to repent and change so you can move closer toward God's perfect plans and will for your life.

Operating in the prophetic is like walking up to a solid wall, where you have no idea what is behind it, and putting a periscope over the wall and thus viewing what is behind it. It's seeing into the unseen, hearing the unheard, and knowing the unknown. It is like a soldier on the battlefield having the ability to tap into the cameras in the satellites that orbit the earth, linking into a real-time feed of images and video footage to reveal all the surrounding territories. This will enable not only the soldier but his or her entire squad or battalion to be aware of objectives, threats, supplies, resources, and even places of safety.

THE PROPHET: GOD'S MOUTHPIECE

God has chosen to speak through His selected prophets at various times and in various ways since Adam and Eve evacuated the Garden of Eden. Since that day, God's interaction and voice to humanity changed. The day Adam sinned, all of us became disconnected from God, whereas prior to that, God would come to the Garden in the cool of the day, every day, and talk with Adam and Eve.

I imagine that in the purity of that sinless world, the conversations extended to every aspect of the imagination. Imagine hearing God's unlimited heart on every matter in an unrestricted way. Now God communicates to us through a veiled form in comparison to what took place in the Garden of Eden. But for those who still their hearts and focus their ears to hear His voice, we will hear His whispers. There are those whom God has selected over the course of time to be His mouthpieces and representatives to speak to people groups, nations, or even to the entire world.

A prophet is one who is positioned in a place of influence for the right people at the right time, who has been trained by the Spirit of God and with the words of God in his or her mouth. Being positioned in a place of influence does not necessarily mean that there is a social elevation like a minister or a king, but only that God has put His words in his or her mouth. Look at John the Baptist as an example. He was of no social note, but God powerfully used him to pronounce and declare the coming and arrival of Jesus Christ, God's coming Messiah. However, God has His prophets strategically positioned in all facets of life from the courtrooms of royalty, churches, political arenas, the marketplaces of work and business, to everyday life situations.

THE POWER OF THE WORD

In the gospel of John, we read, "In the beginning was the Word, and the Word was with God, and the Word was God" (John 1:1). Then he goes on to write that the Word was made flesh and dwelt among us (John 1:14). The Word, Jesus Christ, is the Father's vehicle to manifest His heart, mind, and truth into the world; Jesus is the road and the only way to Him from where we are.

He is the absolute manifestation of the Word of God. In fact, the Word was so potent and powerful that when it was released from the eternal realm of God's presence to the natural realm in which we live, the Word became a man—Christ Jesus! Prophecy is the mouthpiece or the gateway from which the spoken prophetic word transitions from the spirit realm where God lives to the natural realm where we live.

We have been made in God's image (Genesis 1–3), and so in the same way when God said, "Let there be light" and there was light, we have been designed with life-giving and creative power in our tongues. Not only can we speak life, but there is also the power of death, destruction, and curses if our tongues are not correctly stewarded. That is why we must be careful how we go about speaking. James drives this point home with a powerful illustration.

For we all stumble in many things. If anyone does not stumble in word, he is a perfect man, able also to bridle the whole body. Indeed, we put bits in horses' mouths that they may obey us, and we turn their whole body. Look also at ships: although they are so large and are driven by fierce winds, they are turned by a very small rudder wherever the pilot desires. Even so the tongue is a little member and boasts great things.

See how great a forest a little fire kindles! And the tongue is a fire, a world of iniquity. The tongue is so set among our members that it defiles the whole body, and sets on fire the course of nature; and it is set on fire by hell. For every kind of beast and bird, of reptile and creature of the sea, is tamed and has been tamed by mankind. But no man can tame the tongue. It is an unruly evil, full of deadly poison. With it we bless our God and Father, and with it we curse men, who have been made in the similitude of God. Out of the same mouth proceed blessing and cursing. My brethren, these things ought not to be so. Does a spring send forth fresh water and bitter from the same opening? Can a fig tree, my brethren, bear olives, or a grapevine bear figs? Thus no spring yields both salt water and fresh. (James 3:2–12)

We see from this passage that the same creative and life-giving power that sculpted the universe and every aspect of creation is in each of our mouths. This is why it is so important to grasp the fact that the Father made us in His image. When God breathes and speaks, the prophetic word goes out of your mouths.

The Holy Spirit (the same Spirit who hovered over the face of the deep in Genesis 1) is still waiting for the word of God to be released from our mouths so He can partner in the life-giving creation with us, heaven being released on earth! And when a God-breathed word is released, the Spirit reacts and the Spirit goes forth in power. The Word and the Spirit come together and something is birthed from the spiritual realm into the natural world.

A SOBERING RESPONSIBILITY

The prophet or a person prophesying is not partaking of a casual thing. I don't want to give the idea that it is a scary event, but definitely is not casual. A prophet has been given a sobering responsibility of stewarding what God has spoken and is speaking for a specific time (present, past, or future) or for a specific person. The prophetic word is not to be taken lightly or flippantly like many seem to do today. This is not to paint any bondage on the role, for it is a joyous gift that is meant for the good of the body of Christ.

The apostle Paul said that we are to "pursue love, and desire spiritual gifts, but especially that you may prophesy" (1 Corinthians 14:1). In many situations in the body of Christ today, words are "handed out" so casually, without any soberness or consciousness that it is God's line of communication with us. Every word spoken in God's name really needs to be weighed and tested before it is spoken. Not that I don't have prophecies fail, but we must handle this role as a messenger with a consciousness that we will be responsible and give an account for every word we speak on God's behalf.

When I was young in the prophetic—even sometimes now—I would miss a word. (The truth is that all of us will, and there is grace for that.) But we don't want to be "hit and miss" when it comes to speaking God's word, which is like the blind leading the blind. Presuming to speak on God's behalf is a pretty big presumption. People can have their whole lives directed by one word, and if it wasn't from God we can be partially responsible for the train wreck of their wrong direction or decision.

For instance, I knew of a couple who attended another church and who were prophesied to while they were single that they were to get married. Even though they didn't even like each other, they started dating and got married based on that one word. They even had children. But eventually the marriage fell apart. They based their whole decision to get married on one word that was supposedly from God.

On a side note, this is not to say that God cannot take situations like this and still help us and even bless us. We cannot use excuses like, "It was the false prophetic," to justify decisions like divorce. Once we make a decision to move forward in areas like this, it is then our responsibility to work out our journey with integrity and longevity as led by the Lord.

Speaking for God is a weighty responsibility that we must consider. Like pastors, a prophet has a responsibility over the words and people to which they declare, "Thus saith the Lord," or "God is saying over you"—these things must not be flippant. If you find yourself in a situation where you feel you were led in the wrong direction by an apparent or presumed prophetic word, don't blame the prophet or the messenger, take responsibility yourself for the decision to act on the word.

The Bible is clear on the instruction in Philippians 2:12, that you are to "work out your own salvation with fear and trembling." In other words, don't do things because someone else said to do them; take every prophetic word or plan to the Lord and seek His confirmation so you know whether or not it's really His will and not someone else's or your own will.

The Bible also says, "Do not believe every spirit, but test the spirits, whether they are of God" (1 John 4:1), and "in the mouth of two or three witnesses let every word be established" (Matthew 18:16). We cannot blame people for making wrong decisions, even if those people are the ones who prophesied to us; it is ultimately our responsibility.

If you find yourself in this position, then I would encourage you to seek God and never be hasty in following a word from someone just because they say it is from God. Rather, seek godly counsel from stable people who have character and longevity with the Lord. And, most importantly, don't be influenced by your emotions. Declaring God's word is a serious thing indeed, and likewise responding to God's prophetic word given through an individual should be tested and weighed. Just because prophets are God's mouthpieces doesn't mean they don't miss it from time to time.

CHAPTER 3

LEARNING TO MOVE IN THE PROPHETIC

When I was eighteen, God spoke to me over a thirty-day period during that summer, each day giving me a new Scripture relating to being a prophet and the gift of prophecy. I was new to this and barely knew anything about the prophetic, if anything at all. I was raised in a conservative church where we looked at Bible end-time prophecy in great depth, but the office and function of a prophet was something I never really saw in operation or even had any concept of.

I was not filled with the Holy Spirit yet, but I knew that God was telling me that He was going to make me a prophet. But I had no idea at all what that looked like or even how to get there. There was just simply no one in my life whom I had ever seen walk as a prophet, or even in the prophetic, so I had no picture of what God was calling me into. All I could see was the old Hollywood produced movies of a Charlton Heston–style actor playing a prophet with a large beard, a one-piece robe, and a long walking stick, walking down the dusty main street into town, shouting judgment and condemnation against the people in the name of God. As you can imagine, I was not totally clear on what God meant. But I was sure about what He was telling me.

During those thirty days, one of the Scriptures God gave me to confirm what He was saying was 1 Samuel 10:6. It says, "Then the Spirit of the LORD will come upon you, and you will prophesy with them and be turned into another man." I was not familiar with the presence of God or the way God speaks, but I knew that God was clearly showing me something.

I held this promise in my spirit, knowing that God had a special and unique call on my life. Three years later I had an encounter and was filled with the Holy Spirit in a youth meeting while on a trip in a different part of the country. A year after that, I had a chance meeting through a few of my friends with a man who would mentor me for a time. There was a progression showing up in my life in which it was apparent that God was leading and unfolding the pathway of His promises to me. I served this man for a season and I gleaned from his experience and anointing.

Learning to move in the prophetic is the practice of being sensitive in your spirit to what God wants to say or do in a given moment of time. Sometimes we need people to come alongside us, to teach us how to discern the voice of God. Through this man I learned how to move in the prophetic gift that was already placed on me, I learned how to better discern and test the spirits, and I grew in the realm of the prophetic during that season of my life.

We are not called to be blind followers, but followers who see and pay attention to what we are being taught. God has placed people in our lives as mentors and spiritual fathers and mothers, some for a season and others are lifelong. But we must always remember that the Holy Spirit has to be our primary source of teaching and leading when it comes to following His voice.

WORSHIP IS A GATEWAY INTO THE SPIRIT REALM

The prophetic realm is a mystical realm indeed. It can be tapped into at almost any time. For instance, in worship (whether alone in your room, in a gathering with your church, or at an event) the atmosphere can suddenly change, something happens, and the room is suddenly filled with an electric anointing—God's presence fills the environment. I have become sensitive to this, as it is God's Spirit shifting the direction of the meeting.

This is something we must all become sensitive to, as it is never a person in charge of any meeting or gathering. Ministers are merely facilitators of God's agenda. The second a leader or minister ignores the agenda of what God is doing in the room or atmosphere, religion has taken hold of that meeting and God's Spirit is quenched.

It is always Jesus, the Holy Spirit, and Father God who are in charge at the head of the body of Christ, and so we must learn to submit to His agenda and His will in the flow of His Spirit. When this happens, the atmosphere takes on a different feel or direction, which is usually a signal that God wants to speak or reveal something supernatural in that moment. There is always God's timing and order to these things, so just because we sense what God is doing in the room does not mean we are the ones God wants to act on it.

Discernment of what is happening and authorization to act are two different things, and discerning a prophetic prompting does not authorize you in any way to step out to disrupt a meeting. This is why Paul instructed us in 1 Corinthians 14:40, "Let all things be done decently and in order." He is not shutting down our gifts, but He is making way for submitted decency and order in His kingdom on earth so that chaos does not break out in church services and meetings.

When I was young in my prophetic gift, I was in a meeting with one of the world's most well-known evangelists. We were worshiping the Lord, and a moment of stillness came into the room as God was apparently moving by His Spirit. The room became intensely filled—I felt the air become electric and shift into the distinct presence I know well. The Spirit of God had just entered and He was about to speak. And so I began to listen with my spirit, eagerly knowing that something was about to happen much like it had happened in meetings and in my room when no one was looking so many times before. I heard a distinct and clear message in my spirit from the Spirit of God.

I asked God if it was for me to say or if someone else was meant to deliver it. But I felt a restraint from the Holy Spirit, so I held it back. Just a few seconds later, another prophet in the room stood up and began to deliver the exact message to the evangelist that I was sensing. I learned a lot that day. So many times we can hear into the spirit realm where God is constantly speaking, but what we must discover is whether or not we are the ones meant to disclose what we heard.

The Scriptures tell us in Ecclesiastes 8:5, "A wise man's heart discerns both time and judgment." Not only must we discern what God is saying in a moment or a specific situation, but we must also discern His timing on when we are to speak or act. Hastiness has been the downfall of many in this area, as it not only leads to shame and embarrassment, but it also leads to moments of discredit. The prophetic really does require the integrity of consistent character.

Always identify whom God has appointed in the situation as the lead role and submit to his or her direction and leading around these matters. For instance, it is a different matter if you are visiting or new to a church and discern a prophetic moment, than if you are, for instance, in the leadership of that church. In many ways, the prophetic is facilitating and stewarding what God wants to do and say. It is stewarding His direction.

Walking in this realm so that you can hear what He is communicating comes from being a friend of God, learning what He likes and how He likes to do things, and really importantly, being sensitive enough to hear His voice and feel Him move. In these moments, it is important not to perform but to locate in your spirit what God wants to say or do through you. It may be to give a prophetic word, it may be a prophetic sound, or it may be a prophetic dance or act. Whatever the case, responding to God will bring freedom, breakthrough, vision, hope, and dreams.

Worship is a powerful gateway into the spirit realm. David's playing of the harp bought peace and liberty to Saul because David's worship opened a portal of God's presence into the palace and Saul's demonic oppression had to flee. In the same way, when we worship God in such a way that the heavens open up, we experience freedom and liberty because the Spirit of the Lord has come. And when He comes into worship, He will often (but not always) speak. In my observations of God, it is often through one of His children that He speaks, but not always.

Let's look at a few avenues through which the prophetic is delivered to us from God's world.

THE SONG OF THE LORD

I was on my church worship team for many years, and during that time I learned the way the Spirit of God would descend into an atmosphere of pure worship. The Spirit of the Lord would come on someone on the worship team, and that person would begin to sing a song that wasn't pre-rehearsed or prewritten; it was a new song that came straight from heaven. We called this the song of the Lord.

The song of the Lord can have many faces. It can be the bridegroom singing His love over people as found in the Song of Solomon, or it can be the strong breaker anointing with the face of the lion warrior bringing breakthrough into people's lives and shattering strongholds. The song of the Lord can be the prophetic voice speaking guidance and direction, it can be the voice of repentance on behalf of a people, or it can be the voice of the creative mouth of God speaking things into being. Not only that, but the song of the Lord can also be the voice of the bride calling out to the heart of God. This is truly a beautiful aspect of the prophetic nature being expressed in the midst of God's people.

If I could summarize how this works, I would say that the greatest moments of revelation in which the song of the Lord has come has been sparked from deep, intimate moments of worship in which the heart of God has been stirred in such a way that He has desired to respond or speak into certain situations. Providing a space for God to speak and respond is equally important. Worshipers need to pause and allow moments of stillness and quietness of heart to make way for these special opportunities to hear God's heart expressed and sung through someone who took the care and time to listen to Him.

I have intently watched the kingdom being fully expressed during these moments. I have seen God's presence come and bring deliverance, healing, salvation, and breakthrough without a preacher or an altar call when God is given the opportunity and platform to sing His song through us in moments of worship.

Take time to learn and steward this amazing expression of the song of the Lord, for this is truly a beautiful aspect of the prophetic nature being expressed.

THE WORD OF THE LORD

The word of the Lord is the spoken statement on God's behalf that can be uttered through many different perspectives. It is something that appears almost as a phenomenon, and carries weight and the presence of God when spoken. The Bible says in 1 Peter 4:11, "If anyone speaks, let him speak as the oracles of God." We cannot just fabricate "God said" statements, which would be flippant and playing dangerously with people's lives; it would be disrespecting God. But as we seek God and He speaks to us, we can represent Him as a mouthpiece or a messenger and deliver His message to whom it's addressed. We are just the messengers. In fact, actually Jesus lived the same way. He claimed that He only spoke the words the Father was speaking (John 12:49).

The word of the Lord is just that—God's words being heard and conveyed. It is one of the functions of a prophet, and one that every prophet and prophetic person must learn to become accurate in and deliver well. The word of the Lord has changed my life. It is a powerful delivery of God's plans, instruction, lifesaving warnings, and wisdom. It is a vehicle through which a new set of visionary future purpose and destiny is unveiled, where dreams are expressed from the womb of God's planning over our lives. Many times I have either been saved from imminent disaster or given the remedy to get out of a situation in which the enemy had sought to ensnare me. Endless times my heart has been strengthened knowing that God was with me and for me and that I was pleasing Him with my life decisions and heart conditions.

Countless times I have had strangers ,who knew nothing about me or my journey, tell me things they could never have known in the natural, reminding me of the things God had promised me years earlier, or I would receive fresh vision and promise filling my heart with hope and joy. Never underestimate the power and potency of life-giving vision that a person can receive when the word of the Lord is released.

DREAMS AND VISIONS

Visions are another avenue that God often uses to speak what is on His heart. They include dreams, visions, and spirit realm experiences. It's like seeing still pictures or movies in your mind's eye—with your eyes closed or even sometimes open—except the pictures or movies are messages or insights from God. When God releases visions, it takes you into the imagery of what God wants to convey to either you or a particular person. Sometimes the imagery is clear, but at other times it can be mystical and cryptic, needing interpretation like in the times of Daniel and Joseph.

I love visions because they immerse you into the heartbeat of the message. Visions add a third dimension to what God is saying. For example, instead of a sentence, you are able to see details and imagery around what God is speaking or revealing, adding more depth to it. There have been times in which God has come to me with visions and the details of the visions have played out over several years. Based on the vision, I was able to navigate and make decisions that kept me safe during that season.

Visions are an amazing way for not just instructional revelation, but also for a revealing of the heart and love of the Father. I have had visionary encounters in which God has revealed certain aspects of Himself to me, which have impacted me so deeply that my life has been changed and influenced by what was shown to me in those moments.

PROPHETIC ART

Prophetic art is such a powerful reflection of the creative nature of the Creator. It is an inherent trait for us to be like our Father, after all, for we were made in His image and likeness. And prophetic art is just another way in which we can convey His heartbeat. Many times prophets have a deeply creative aspect to their makeup.

Prophetic art is an expressive art form whereby an artist can translate what the Lord is showing him or her onto a medium, like canvas, paper, or clay. It has become popular in some churches that selected prophetic artists can draw or paint while worship is taking place. This can be a pictorial way where God can communicate a message from His heart to His people.

There is an instance of this in the Bible. God instructed Moses to construct a bronze serpent and erect it on a pole in front of the people. This was done at a time when God sent snakes into the camp because of the peoples' unbelief and sin, and the snakes were killing the people. Once the brazen serpent was erected on a pole, however, the people who looked upon it were healed and saved (Numbers 21:4–9). This was a simple act that God used powerfully. An artisan worked with his or her creative gift and coupled it with the prophetic command, and all who saw it were saved.

Another example of this can be seen in Genesis 30, where we read about the prophetic act in which Jacob put rods and strips of bark in front of the herds of sheep and goats as they mated, and in their water source. He had an agreement with Laban that all the speckled and spotted animals would be Jacob's, but all the other animals would be Laban's. As Jacob put these rods and strips of bark in front of the herd, many of the sheep and goats were born speckled and spotted and became his property according to his agreement with Laban. His prophetic act, which looked like expressive art, caused faith to be activated and God responded. The result was that Jacob became rich with livestock.

The dance of the Lord is another way form of prophetic expression and art, and another way that God can communicate with His people. This is a physical outworking with actions or dancing of something God wants to express. Sometimes that can look like an actual dancer and sometimes it can be a simple action on behalf of whomever God is speaking to. For instance, there have been times when I have been in the presence of God and have started to motion my body or hands in a certain way, which is a sign of what God is going to be doing. It can be as simple as a cutting-type action, symbolically cutting chains or bonds that have been holding people back, or it could be a dance that tells a story or paints a picture of what God is saying. Your body can be used for prophetic expressions and declarations as well.

The truth is that God is such a creative expresser that He will often use prophetic art and artists of varying forms to convey a message or an insight into His heart and kingdom.

It is an amazing thing when a seer is able to draw, paint, or recreate on paper or via media what they have seen from looking into God's realm. There have been times when I have had detailed visions for people, and trying to explain the exact details was a challenge for me, so instead I sketched the visions for these people and given them an illustrated prophetic message. They had something tangible in order to constantly remind them of God's promise. It's great for someone receiving the word or vision to have insight into the picture that God has shown the prophetic messenger. It's also great as prophetic art will last a long time and act as a continual reminder of God's destiny for that person.

If we are to pursue the spiritual gifts, especially the gift of prophecy, then we must be a people who learn how to move in the prophetic realm. God longs to speak to us and through us, but are we willing to listen?

CHAPTER 4

PROPHETIC PROMISES AND OPPORTUNITIES

God can open a door of opportunity for a person, offering him or her a new season, a breakthrough, or a blessing. But the person's heart will determine whether or not he or she enters through the door. The blessing is a mere conditional promise that is given by God, not a guaranteed reality. It is likened to the twelve spies going into the Promised Land of Canaan, which we read about in Numbers 13.

God had promised this land to His people generations before, and yet when the time came to possess the promise, the children of Israel were gripped with fear because of the great challenges that stood between their current position and their God-given inheritance. We learn from this that a promise is never an automatic guarantee. Rather, a promise from God is an invitation to partner with God, an opportunity that requires two parties in a covenant, involving both man and God. The opportunity presented through the prophetic is not guaranteed but conditional, dependent on faith and obedience.

A prophetic word is simply an invitation to agree with God's dream for and over your life, and then move toward that blessing. Moving toward the blessing looks like acts of faith and obedience in the direction of God's promise for your life.

MOVING INTO THE PROMISES OF GOD

My experience walking with God and watching Him design both my own and other people's destinies has led me to have a firm belief that He designs a future for each and every one of us, an ideal plan that He has perfected from His perspective. We can catch just a glimpse of God's dream and plan over each person's destiny if we read Jeremiah 29:11. God, through the prophet Jeremiah, declares, "For I know the thoughts that I think toward you, says the LORD, thoughts of peace and not of evil, to give you a future and a hope."

Even though God has a plan to give us a future and a hope, we have a choice to make. That plan is an invitation to inquire, find out, agree with, and then line up with His path for our lives. That's why I sometimes refer to prophetic words and promises simply as opportunities. They are promises, yes, but ones that need to be agreed on by faith and demonstrated in actions in order to inherit them. A good way to see a prophetic word is to see it as an invitation to agree with God the Father and walk through a door and down a new pathway that God has secretly prepared for you ahead of time.

For instance, God may have spoken to you that He has called you to become a millionaire or successful businessperson to fund the kingdom. That doesn't mean it is guaranteed and will happen; rather, that word is an invitation to agree with His perfect will for your life. Think of it as a conditional promise. To see the promise come to pass, you will need to put actions with your faith. That isn't a cue card to begin striving for, but rather an invitation to begin partnering in the work. And when I say "work," I am referring to whatever God has shown you to do with your hands that will become an avenue through which blessings from God flow to you and through you.

That is not to say that God cannot bless you outside of your job or your business. But there are plenty of Scriptures that indicate hard work brings blessing, while laziness does not. Many teach that blessing and prosperity fall out of the sky, and on some levels they are correct, for "every good and perfect gift is from above, and comes down from the Father of lights, with whom there is no variation or shadow of turning" (James 1:17). However, there is a balance to this, as the Scripture also tells us that faith without works is dead (James 2:17).

To paint a picture of contrast, God could speak to a person who is significantly overweight that they were going to lose weight, and that person believed God and told everyone this and yet ate cheeseburgers and had soda ten times a day. Insane, right? We know that God's promise of him or her losing weight isn't going to automatically come as a gift from God that falls out of the sky—he or she is going to have to work out the promise of God, partner with Him in His invitation, and do some hard work in order to lose the weight. That person is going to have clean out his or her fridge and fill it with salads and lean foods and eat in accordance with the promise they have received from God.

This is why James said that faith without works is dead. We must combine our faith with our works, not just merely rely on our prophetic faith. There are so many Scriptures around faith and works to demonstrate this principle of God's kingdom. The writer of Proverbs said, "The hand of the diligent will rule, but the lazy man will be put to forced labor" (Proverbs 12:24), and, "In all toil there is profit, but mere talk leads to poverty" (Proverbs 14:23 ESV). And Paul wrote to Timothy, "The hardworking farmer must be first to partake of the crops" (2 Timothy 2:6), and then he wrote again, "And let us not grow weary while doing good, for in due season we shall reap if we do not lose heart" (Galatians 6:9).

God expects us to work toward a harvest of prosperity and blessing. The problem with most of the first-world churches is that there is a strong expectation of entitlement, which is a misconception of the way God does things. There is inheritance and access to heavenly resources in the kingdom of God, but there isn't a self-centered, me-focused entitlement perspective to God's promises. Most Christians have an expectation with prophetic words that God has dispatched the prophetic package, and all they need to do is sit back on their sofas and wait for the knock on the door with the delivery of the promise. But it really does not work like this. God wants us to combine works with our faith.

A farmer who believes that God told him he is going to have a massive crop of corn, doesn't just sit back and expect it to happen. He expects it to happen, yes, but he also works toward it. The entitlement tendency would cause farmer Mike to say, "I believe God has told me that I am going to have a huge crop this year, so that's God's job. I'm going to wait for Him to do it and sit on my sofa and watch TV." This is faith without works, otherwise known as an entitlement mentality.

From the neighboring property, farmer John says, "God spoke to me about having a really large harvest this year. Now what do I need to do to prepare for that?" John will then ensure the ground is tilled, the soil has the right nutrients, the sowing is carried out correctly, and that watering happens exactly when it needs to. He will also make sure the pruning during the growing period happens, the right fertilizer is being used, and finally that the harvest is taking place at the right time. John will need to ensure that he has enough harvesting workers, machines, and vehicles, and that he has room to store it all after it is taken from the field. If *any* one point in this process is not carried out, or carried out incorrectly or at the wrong time, then this could sabotage John's harvest. In addition to the word that he received from God, John has become extremely diligent to do all he knows to do to ensure the fruitfulness and abundance of that crop.

This is faith and expectation that something good is coming, and it is followed by directly related actions and works that prepare the environment for that which one is believing. Farmer John has done all he possibly could to correctly position himself for God's word, and then the rest is left up to God, for Him to breathe on his crop. Farmer Mike, on the other hand, has failed miserably by neglecting to put actions with his faith.

James told his reader, "I will show you my faith *by* my works" (James 2:18). We must always put more emphasis on what we do in response to what we believe rather than what we "declare in faith." The reason I say this is because many declare the promises of God and do nothing in faith to usher in those promises. Faith requires action, and in most cases so does the prophetic word that has been declared in faith.

When God speaks to us, we are invited to look at and consider what our responsibility looks like to prepare for and position ourselves for what God has shown. There's a saying that salvation is free for all, but it will cost you. Much the same is true as we partner with God's prophetic promises. We will have the vision, which is given for free, but we will need to add actions to our faith in order to obtain the vision and walk into it (which will cost you).

THE POTENCY OF GOD'S WORDS

It is my prayer that we truly begin to grasp the potency of God's words, and just how important His words are in His own eyes. You see, if God broke His word just once, then He would cease to be perfect and cease to be God as we know Him to be. Understanding the power of God's words gives us an anchor point to which we can lock and ground all of our prophetic pursuits. Understanding that He is faithful and keeps His promises, should cause us to be faithful to do our part to see God's prophetic promises come to pass.

SUBMISSION BRINGS CLARITY

Generally, I have experienced the greatest moments in my walk with God when I have been able to see and agree with what God has been doing because I have been submitted to Him the most. Submission brings clarity. We walk through the doors of opportunity that God opens up when we choose to see them and be open to God's best for us, no matter what that looks like. Being humble and submitted actually allows the eyes of our spirits to be opened to understand more of what is on God's heart in a given situation or prophetic moment. Understanding, even in adverse and hard situations, allows us to better partner with God and walk out the journey between the promise and the actual realizing of that word.

I have experienced God's clarifying voice many times as I have humbled my heart and submitted to who God is and what He is doing in my life. I humbled and submitted my life to God, putting myself into a position of making life less about my agenda and priorities and more about what pleases Him. It was in those moments where I experienced closer intimacy, where His voice seemed so much brighter and louder and clearer.

When I was twenty-four, I had been in business for four years. I had a business partner who had robbed me and fled the country after stripping the business overnight. I came to the end of myself, broken and pretty hopeless. I didn't know what to do, and life was looking bleak and intimidating—I was afraid. That often happens after you lose everything you have and then a whole lot more. I had not only lost everything, but I had gone into debt for $750,000 as a result of this man stealing from the company.

I took a few days and went up into the mountains with an agenda to fall on my face and cry out to God. When I got up there, I simply poured my heart out to the Lord through a lot of tears and laid all my future before Him. "What do I do, God? What's Your plan from here?"

Over the following days, God clearly and specifically downloaded what I needed to do, and along with that came a blueprint from which all my debts were then paid off. In fact, I prospered more than ever before. But the journey from the place of hearing His voice and instruction wasn't easy, but I followed it, and it worked out well for me.

God's prophetic promises are not always guaranteed, but they are invitations and opportunities for you to mix your faith with action, and partner with God to see those things come to pass. God has given us tremendous promises and opportunities, inviting us to mix our actions with our faith. Will you follow His invitation?

CHAPTER 5

PROPHETIC STEWARDSHIP

Do you remember the parable of the talents that Jesus talked about in Matthew 25:14–30? That was a story about stewardship, of stewardship carried out well and carried out badly. Though the parable had to do with money in particular, there are elements that can relate to stewarding the prophetic realm as well, for we are called to steward all that has been entrusted to us, both earthly gifts and spiritual gifts.

Being a good steward of the prophetic is a combination of being obedient to and accurate with the word of God, while also expressing humility in its delivery (as well as in your life and character). Behaving humbly when prophesying in itself is not sufficient; people need to see a consistent lifestyle of humility, holiness, and integrity in your life—not just momentary acts of it. Not only do you need to be obedient and accurate in giving what God has impressed upon your heart, and not only do you need to live a life of humility, but you also need to be grounded in boldness in the word and Spirit of the Lord.

There is good stewardship and there is bad stewardship when it comes to the prophetic. When we look at the flaws in bad stewardship, however, then godly stewardship can become more apparent. I find that defining what something is not often reveals even more clearly what it actually looks like, for the light is appreciated so much more when it shines through the darkness.

So let's look at a few crucial areas that we need to pay attention to in our own lives as sons and daughters of the King as we walk out the prophetic journey.

A LACK OF ACCURACY AND CONSISTENCY

A lack of accuracy and consistency in conveying what God has shown or spoken is an obvious sign in a person's life or ministry that stewardship is not being walked out rightly. One thing that really bothers me is seeing a slow evolution of a prophetic word. It's like a spiritual game of telephone that kids used to play. Someone starts off with a word or a sentence, and then he or she whispers it into the next person's ear, and it is passed from person to person across the room until the last person delivers what they received. Most of the time, the message will have drastically evolved—it's quite entertaining how off track the message became as it went from person to person.

A prophetic word goes through a gradual evolution as God gives a word or a vision and it is grasped by a person. Then, whether right away or over time as they retell it, they begin to change details, meanings, or applications here and there. Slowly but surely the prophetic message begins to take on another form or shape altogether. But this should not be so! Understanding how easily this happens has caused me to take stewarding God's words very seriously, because when God speaks to me, it is my solemn and sober duty to relay exactly and only what He has shown me—nothing more, nothing less.

Prophets who change or alter words and visions when they deliver them, risk "playing God." This is due to a lack of the fear of the Lord in their hearts, or to put it differently, it is due to a lack of a healthy respect for God's authority and position in their lives. Did you know that the scribes who made copies of the Torah (the first five books of the Old Testament) would write every character on a parchment by hand as they meticulously and accurately copied the original version they had? If they so much as made a mistake of one incorrect word, they had to discard the whole scroll and start over again.

The scribes who conveyed an accurate word from God held it in the most serious of matters. If you look at the end of the book of Revelation, there is a statement that says:

> *For I testify to everyone who hears the words of the*
> *prophecy of this book: If anyone adds to these things, God*
> *will add to him the plagues that are written in this book;*
> *and if anyone takes away from the words of the book of*
> *this prophecy, God shall take away his part from the Book*

*of Life, from the holy city, and from the things which are
written in this book. (Revelation 22:18–19)*

This is one of the last phrases that God selected and positioned at the end of the Bible. What people say at the conclusion of a conversation can sometimes carry the most weight, giving structure or importance to the whole conversation. Here we see that God chose to add this weighty instruction not to add to or take away from the words in the Book. This also reveals God's stance and standard for people stewarding the gift of prophecy.

How does this happen? How do words gradually change over time? I have spent a great deal of time marveling at how this happens, and I have reduced the cause down to one of four reasons in each circumstance.

First, this can happen through carelessness and a lack of attention to detail in which the prophetic person or prophet has become dulled in his or her standards. This dulling can be due to a lack of real maturity in the God-given gift or in his or her walk with God. A prophet is not called to be tardy, but to have a high standard of truth and hold fast to it as a crucial and structural pillar in his or her life. If you are seeking the Lord, and God's hand is on your life, then time can remedy this. Allow these to develop maturity in your life so that you are not naive to the ways of God and His standards.

Second, it can be because the prophet's fear of man is greater than his or her fear of God. The Word of God clearly instructs us that "the fear of the LORD is the beginning of wisdom ..." (Proverbs 9:10). When a prophet cares more about pleasing God and accurately conveying what the Spirit of God has revealed through a healthy respect for God, then he or she is someone we are more inclined to trust, and someone God is more likely to trust with His messages.

Anybody can deliver a word of blessing, but it takes a real prophetic person to deliver an "uncomfortable and confronting" word accurately and in the right spirit. Today, if you are serious about your call, then build into your life the fear of the Lord, for it will cause you to depart from evil that would otherwise want you to betray the accurate word of the Lord and misrepresent God.

The third way a prophetic word can evolve over time is that the prophet has not harnessed his or her emotions and becomes overly emotive in either a positive or negative way, in either blessing or judgment toward the person, because of like or dislike toward them. I have seen words get watered down to lessen the convicting blow and lose all of their effect simply because the prophet wanted to be gentle on the recipient. And I have also seen the word gain a harsh edge on it when delivered with added prejudice by a prophet who had a dislike toward a specific person.

When you stand before people to prophesy, especially people whom you have feelings toward, whether feelings of dislike or warmth, remember you are not standing and speaking on your own behalf. You must practice putting your feelings on the shelf and operating as a mouthpiece for the Lord. Not giving vent to your feelings is a discipline that is learned through practice and submission to the Spirit of God,

The final reason I can see for why words tend to change over time is that some people are so familiar with the prophetic that they have no reverence for the sacredness of delivering a message from God's heart. And so because of their own desire to get approval from people, to manipulate them, or to position themselves for their own priorities, in their own minds they become the source of the prophetic power rather than humble vessels of the Lord.

This is the same deception into which Lucifer fell. He was so close to the throne of God that he eventually started to take credit for the worship that was coming past him to the Lord, and he became delusional, thinking he was the recipient of it. Because of his talented gifting and apparent beauty, he forgot that he was a created being made to serve and glorify God on the throne, not be a god himself. This tendency to become familiar with the prophetic must be guarded with all diligence by every prophet who serves the Lord so that glory is not taken as our own—it belongs entirely to the Lord. Never allow yourself to become familiar with the prophetic nature of God, for there should always be awe and wonder in your heart toward it.

None of these motives or causes are okay. We must conform to the image of Christ, who said, "The Son can do nothing of Himself, but what He sees the Father do; for whatever He does, the Son also does in like manner" (John 5:19). There must be a right representation of the heavenly pattern that is conveyed by those walking in the prophetic.

Now look again to the Scriptures. Jesus taught in the Sermon on the Mount:

*Do not think that I came to destroy the Law or the
Prophets. I did not come to destroy but to fulfill. For
assuredly, I say to you, till heaven and earth pass away,
one jot or one tittle will by no means pass from the law till
all is fulfilled. Whoever therefore breaks one of the least of
these commandments, and teaches men so, shall be called
least in the kingdom of heaven; but whoever does and
teaches them, he shall be called great in the kingdom of
heaven. (Matthew 5:17–19)*

Jesus is referring to the Law here, which was the Word of God prophetically spoken to the people of Israel. God's perspective is still like this toward prophecy today. When God speaks to you as a prophet or prophetess, you do not have *any* rights to alter or edit what He says. If you do so, then you are taking a big risk in operating in divination and misrepresenting the heart of the Father, either in a word of blessing or judgment. And if you do twist what God has spoken to you, if you alter or evolve these heavenly messages, then you are in danger of God taking exception and teaching you not to play god in people's lives. Your job is to represent Him, not be Him! I pray that you would allow holy soberness to overwhelm your life and walk with God so that you can walk wisely in this arena before God and before others. And as you are faithful with the prophetic measure that you have been given to steward, God will increase it. I have learned this principle and established it as a pillar in my life. As a result, God has brought me before all kinds of great men and women.

If you cannot convey to people around your day-to-day life exactly what is told to you, then how will you not be overwhelmed when standing before a famous individual with a word they might not want to hear, or not say more than you should when bringing a word of encouragement or blessing to someone of that caliber? If you are faithful with the little, Jesus said, then you will be qualified to be made a ruler over much (Luke 16:10). Many prophets find themselves overwhelmed by people's stardom or fame and fail to rightly represent God's message.

Look at Joseph and Daniel, for example. These two stood before the greatest rulers of their time and had to deliver words and visions that were not encouraging words of blessings. Each of their journeys and challenging situations made way for a maturity in their lives, which prepared them for the time when they would be required to stand before kings and deliver judgments, knowing that displeasing a king could result in their execution. Sometimes the prophetic mantle will walk you into situations that you do not want to go with messages that you do not want to deliver. But remember they are not your messages; you are merely a messenger for the King. Be faithful and do not fear them. Fear only God.

When God called Jeremiah to the office of the prophet, God ask Jeremiah what he saw. Jeremiah replied, "I see an almond tree," to which God replied, "You have seen correctly." This is both a lesson and a warning for all of us who would move in the prophetic gifting.

God showed Jeremiah something and then asked him what he had just seen. After Jeremiah replied, God confirmed that he was seeing correctly, implying that there was a wrong way to see and a right way to see. The almond tree does not flower or blossom in spring like most trees; it flowers in winter. This is a perfect insight into the nature of God's prophetic ways. God speaks life into a dead season. A tree flowering in winter is like a prophetic word coming to you in a season of bareness, when everything in your current season speaks against that promise of living and bearing fruit. The word of the Lord will *always* challenge your environment and circumstances.

This is where many prophetic people are tempted to compromise in the word they have received because it is contradictory to the current situation. All of your natural reasoning is going to war against the statement that is coming out of the Spirit. We must hold firm to the prophecies, which are given; we use these words to wage war. Never soften or water down a word or vision because of fear of what people will think; be a good steward and the capacity of the prophetic gift will increase in your life. Don't doctor a word to be better because you like a person or make it harsh because you don't like a person. Two plus two is four, it's not three because you don't get along with a person and it's not five because he or she is your best friend.

God is looking for just prophets and prophetic people who are not looking for personal gain in what they are ministering. If we look at the story of Elisha and his servant Gehazi in 2 Kings 5:20–27, we read that the prophet Elisha was offered payment for his services, but he would not accept it. Then Gehazi chased down the man who offered money and secretly tried to obtain it. It is my belief that Gehazi was supposed to be a great prophet of Israel, like his master

Elisha, but he failed a test of integrity and was bought with money. As a result, Gehazi became a leper and ceased to be Elisha's servant.

We can see the same sin occurring in Number 22:5–35 with the prophet Balaam. Balaam's greed was the same as Gehazi's—they both thought the gift was for sale. We must never forget the gift belongs to God and is for God and His glory. Ask the Holy Spirit to train and discipline you to fine-tune your gift and character to maintain accuracy throughout your life. Don't allow excitement, emotions, or pride to alter what you are supposed to deliver in pure form.

A LACK OF INTEGRITY

A lack of integrity is a huge reputation killer and can break down confidence in the authenticity of prophetic gifts as well. The Bible says that "a good name is more desirable than great riches ..." (Proverbs 22:1). Integrity is doing what you say and saying what you do. It's walking with consistency and honor. Integrity is honesty and transparency.

People value the prophetic and what it brings to the table. However, at times prophetic people can easily lose grasp of the perspective of just how weighty their role is and what it represents. It is a sobering and awesome thing to be operating as a mouthpiece for the King of heaven. People who receive these messages and declarations will often study and observe the "messenger" over time to see if they are the real deal. As a prophetic person, the way you live and treat people is equally as important as what you have said because it validates the authenticity of what was delivered.

For instance, if there was the purest mineral water in a large tank and you wanted to drink it, you would be less inclined to put it into a cup that has been soiled in the mud and dirt, right? You would want to drink that water from a clean cup that wasn't going to contaminate the water. No one wants to drink from soiled vessels. In much the same way, integrity is a way that keeps your vessel clean so that others observing you are able to drink the clean water of God's prophetic messages that flow through you.

A person walking in integrity does not have a special prophetic moment and then the following day act as though they don't even have a relationship with God. They are consistent when no one is watching them, and when the whole world is observing them.

The same also applies to walking with stability in your life. Being great one day and then in chaos the following by a life of sporadic, mental, emotional, or spiritual instability will be a red flag for most people when it comes to receiving a prophetic word. It would be like taking financial advice from someone who has been bankrupt twenty times. It's not wise. Thankfully God is always ready to heal and help us through and out of our times of instability and establish Himself into the center of our lives. Allow that process to take place so that when you do step out in your prophetic gifts, you have credibility and character that can be trusted.

A LACK OF HUMILITY

Without humility, it is hard for prophetic people to be taken seriously by those who are discerning. There's almost nothing worse than an arrogant prophet.

It would have certainly appeared that when Joseph was young, his lack of humility got him into trouble when he boasted to his father, Jacob (whose name had been changed to Israel), that everyone in the family would bow down to him. Humility is a sign of true maturity, resulting from a journey walked with God along with a right heart condition. Humility is actually a hallmark of love. It can be seen in 1 Corinthians 13:4–5, where love does not parade itself, it is not puffed up, does not behave rudely, does not seek its own, and it is not provoked.

Have you ever been around an arrogant person who cannot stop bragging about him or herself, or about how great he or she is? These types of people are always pointing out other's flaws and failures. They are not pleasant to be around. And you are much less likely to trust a prophetic word that comes from their lips, as their lack of humility makes it difficult to receive from them. Arrogance has a certain repulsiveness to it—it causes people to back up, distance themselves, and mistrust.

Walking in genuine humility is as important as any other qualification around this office and gift. Without it you will lose trust, credibility, and influence. Pride is the most destructive and blinding of all sins. Don't ever allow yourself to take credit for your gift, for you are merely a carrier of a treasure that God has entrusted to you. The moment you begin to claim responsibility for the outworking of the gifts God has given to you, then you are on a slippery slope. Pride will become conceit and arrogance with a false sense of confidence .

There is something so beautiful about a person who truly leans on Jesus and the Father's voice in everything he or she does. There is something truly beautiful about a person who waits for the Holy Spirit to move, about a person who is so soft and gentle while waiting on the Lord and gives Him all the credit when something takes place prophetically—that person will be trusted with more.

There is a key that attracts the presence of God toward my life. I take a moment and close my eyes, and I picture myself standing before the throne of God. I look up at the bigness and greatness of the Father—how powerful He is, how full of love. I then gain perspective of how big God is and in comparison how small I am, and yet how much love and value He still places on me as His son. It causes a humbling to take place in my soul. I'm not the source; He is the source. This causes me to walk in humility and brokenness, understanding that I am merely delivering a message or prophetic act from His throne.

A LACK OF SUBMISSION AND ACCOUNTABILITY

A lack of submission and accountability in a person's life is a big problem when it comes to moving in the prophetic. Submission validates and increases the anointing. There are no "lone rangers" in the kingdom of heaven. A prophetic person is never a sole agency or law unto him or herself. Unfortunately, many prophets and prophetic people have been rejected and pushed out of church circles because they did not walk in wisdom or they spoke truth into situations that people did not appreciate, and as a result they were shunned. This gave way to too many unhealed people in the prophetic camp, separating themselves from the church body and forming independent mindsets. This is extremely dangerous because it causes a resentment to potentially become established in their hearts, and can cause prophets to have difficulty loving the church body. Only healing and encounters with the love of God can restore this back to the God-design of trust, unity, love, and submission in a healthy community made up of all the differing functions and gifts.

Prophets can only truly operate in the fullness of their calling, gifting, and office when they intentionally and authentically submit themselves under the local church leadership. This includes a home church or any church they may visit. I have seen on many occasions prophets visiting a church they are not a member of and simply assuming spiritual authority and superiority in the room, and they have thundered out great words without permission from the local pastoral authority all in the name of "God said" or the anointing. This is not maturity, but immaturity and rebellion, and an independent spirit. No power can ever flow through division and separation.

One thing I have been taught by the Holy Spirit is that power and authority is only available in and on our lives when we are correctly submitted to spiritual authority.

RELYING ON YOUR GIFT

Prophets who ride their gifts may appear just like every other prophet who waits on and seeks the Lord, but there is something much different about them. What I mean by someone riding his or her gift is that a person has received a gift from God, but he or she relies more on the gift God has given rather than on cultivating a relationship with God, who is the giver of the gift. I am referring to those who are not intimate with God and yet minister as though they are.

The prophetic is a gift of God that is given without strings attached. God will not withdraw the ability for the gift to function in a person's life if he or she is distant from Him or even backslidden. The gift will operate, but it will likely be polluted and will be more strained.

Riding a gift looks like Samson who had a covenant anointing from the Lord, but he became familiar and comfortable with his abilities and forgot the source of his strength and the requirements around his calling. Eventually he became so confident in *his* abilities that he started to take risks and make compromises. He got involved with the world and all of its enticements, thinking that he could hold both and not be burned. He was operating in his gift while not being intimate with or reverently submitted to God (Judges 16).

This is a picture of people who ride their gifts, operating in their gifts without investing in intimacy with the One who gave the gifts. For a prophet, this is a serious danger indeed. If you are not intimate with the Lord, then you will begin to lean on your prophetic gift. I have watched people who are tangled up in gross sin still trying to fool everyone around them by issuing prophetic words. This scares me, as it is so contaminated and obviously not motivated by love. And so I usually discard these prophetic messages as they may or may not be accurate; at best I treat them with caution. Riding your gift also looks like Balaam who actually became so corrupt that he used his gift like a gun for hire and was about to go to war against God's people (Numbers 22).

Never allow yourself to become familiar with your gift or your relationship with God, as they are designed to work together. Think of your gift as a car and your intimacy with God as the fuel for that car. Without intimacy you may be able to drive for a while. Everyone will think that everything is fine for a while, but time will prove that eventually something is going to begin to be compromised in your prophetic integrity. We must ensure that all we do is rooted in the love of God, and it is from this place that all of our ministry flows.

Bring these points up in conversation with Holy Spirit and ask Him, "Are there any of these points that I am lacking in and need Your help with?" Ask Him if there are other areas that have not been listed here that He wants to make you aware of. Allow the

Holy Spirit to teach and mentor you through life's obstacles that have often been sent to fashion and shape you. And in walking through these with His help, you will become all that He made you to be. You will be a man or a woman who has learned how to steward the prophetic well.

CHAPTER 6

THE THREE PROPHETIC GIFTS OF THE SPIRIT

Just before Jesus finished His time with His disciples and then ascended into heaven (Acts 1:9), He said that it was important that He left so that He could send the Holy Spirit to lead, teach, and guide them. Later on, Paul quotes Psalm 68:18 in Ephesians 4:8, and said that when Jesus ascended to the Father, "He gave gifts to men." These gifts are God's abilities that are made available to people, as we are both given them and grow and mature in them.

The gifts of the Spirit are not to be confused with the fruits of the Spirit listed in Galatians 5. The fruits are character-based attributes that the Holy Spirit forms and develops within us, whereas the gifts are special abilities and operations given to us that are empowered by the Spirit of God. The fruits of the Spirit are more associated with the integral and character qualities found in the nature of God, but the gifts have to do with the demonstration of His power and grace in and through our lives.

In this chapter we will primarily focus on three gifts of the Spirit that are prophetically oriented. The three gifts of the Spirit in this category are: words of knowledge, words of wisdom, and prophecy. Let's briefly look at each of these three prophetic gifts. This will serve as an introduction to these gifts, for each of them will be developed more thoroughly in the remaining books in the series. Each of the prophetic facets and roles of the prophet will touch on at least one or more of these three gifts in every instance.

THE WORD OF KNOWLEDGE

The word of knowledge is a Holy Spirit–inspired insight given directly to an individual for various situations in life. It reveals truth with God's supernatural perspective and understanding that human insight cannot access or have any way of knowing, in matters that are both past and present. This could be knowledge about things such as sickness and health, finances and businesses, people and relationships, and situations and circumstances—details that only God can know. There have been times where I have known details that I have not been taught nor told because the Holy Spirit partnered with me through a word of knowledge and downloaded supernatural knowledge of what was taking or had taken place.

This is a powerful gift every believer can and should walk in. It is so crucial to the health of the church because it allows and empowers you to view a specific situation from God's vantage point, to have a divine perspective and insight into situations and decisions in your life, and in some cases into the life of those around you. Ultimately, the word of knowledge will make way for the kingdom of God to expand.

When Jesus met the woman at the well and proceeded to talk to her about her husband, she answered and said that she didn't have a husband. Jesus responded by saying, "You have well said, 'I have no husband,' for you have had five husbands, and the one whom you now have is not your husband; in that you spoke truly" (John 4:17–18). This was a case of Jesus operating in a word of knowledge. He didn't know by natural means that she had had five husbands; it was revealed to Him by the Spirit. In fact, this word of knowledge so powerfully impacted the woman that when she went into town, she told everyone to come and see the man who told her everything she had done!

There have been times when I met people for the first time, and in those initial moments with them I have had divine insight into the not-so-obvious details of their lives that others do not know about. When this happens, it is such a shock to the individual that it captivates his or her attention in a radical way that one becomes acutely aware that God is communicating directly with him or her through this word of knowledge. Through these moments, especially in initial meetings, and God opening such a platform of accuracy, it causes people to listen more intently to what follows. Always understand that the purpose of the word of knowledge is to communicate the heart of God so that a line of communication can be opened, and the person operating in the prophetic can be taken seriously.

Second, the gospel needs to maintain the person's priority. When that person has dropped his or her guard, if even only for a few moments their heart is softened, then it is the time that the seed of salvation must be sown in his or her heart. It is not for you to be built up as a credible prophet, although the more you practice operating in the word of knowledge the better you will become, it is that consistent accuracy brings a certain credibility. However, the goal is that you would be a vessel that humbly presents what God is showing you for the individual or situation and then moves forward in the purposes of God for those people.

Staying humble during and after delivering a word of knowledge is of the utmost importance. We are only messengers of God, not God Himself, so don't take credit from God when we are only operating in a gift that He has given to us.

THE WORD OF WISDOM

The word of wisdom is a specific and direct word breathed out by the Spirit of Wisdom (the same Spirit of Wisdom with which God shaped creation as described in Proverbs 8). This is a supernatural wisdom and understanding that is given by the Spirit, whereby God gives insight into a situation through the eyes of God's wisdom. Receiving a word of wisdom brings safety and godly counsel on how to build or navigate situations and decisions in people's lives, relationships, finances and businesses, ministries, bodies and health, affecting aspects of our personal or corporate worlds as individuals or communities.

We must tap into the Spirit of God and allow His counsel and wisdom to guide the paths of our lives and bring direction and understanding to those whom the Lord has us minister to. There have been times in my business where the word of wisdom has come and averted me from taking on certain projects that seemed to be great opportunities. However, some time later, after not taking the contracts, I would hear of the disasters that took place that would have cost me a great deal of losses. Sometimes when God speaks this type of wisdom, it doesn't make sense until a long time after the instance. It's not until that perspective is present that the wisdom of God's amazing planning becomes apparent.

I find it fascinating that the Holy Spirit can be so gentle and subtle in His delivery of the prophetic words of wisdom and knowledge. For instance, when I am driving out on the freeway, I will get a strong prompting to take a certain route to where I am going, only to find out there was a major traffic jam on the route I would have normally taken. Coincidence? No, I really do not think so. Those who are led by the Spirit are sons and daughters of God. These are moments when the word of wisdom or word of knowledge is not necessarily announced, but just takes place out of pure relationship with the person of God.

Always remember to give credit to the Lord. We are not wise enough to know all these things; it is He who is supplying us with this knowledge. So always stay a humble steward of these things.

PROPHECY

Prophecy is a creative and foretelling gift. Much like the gifts of the word of wisdom and the word of knowledge, the gift of prophecy is given by God for situations which we know nothing about. It is the declaration and creative gift that God uses to materialize His will from the spirit realm into the natural world where we live. This gifting is explained in greater detail throughout the rest of this book.

Prophecy is the gift that God uses to foretell events to come, both in His will and consequences that will come if people do not forsake their sins and humble themselves before Him. It is also a revealer of the schemes and plans of the enemy so that God's children are not caught off guard.

God is not a respecter of persons; He does not have a class system in His kingdom in which some people are worth more than others. He will use anyone who is prepared in heart and willing to allow Him to flow through his or her vessels. We must always remember the high honor it is that God would choose to use us as His mouthpiece through which to flow. It is such a privilege to have His Spirit move on us and cause us to be messengers of His will and words in the earth.

My prayer is that we would always value this fact and that we would always stand in humility, holiness, and reverence of this amazing way that we can both partner with God's Spirit and serve Him in this area and calling of His kingdom. Prophecy is a gift that God offers in His Spirit. It is carried in a resident office by selected individuals called prophets, but prophecy can be operated on certain levels by every believer who chooses to step out and operate and grow into this amazing gift. This is why Paul wrote to the Corinthians, "Pursue love, and desire spiritual gifts, but especially that you may prophesy. ... He who prophesies speaks edification and exhortation and comfort to men" (1 Corinthians 14:1, 3).

CHAPTER 7

THE SEER GIFT

Sometimes a person will look into the spirit realm with his or her physical eyes and see things that are not of this world, or things that would never be possible to see naturally. For instance, there have been moments in my life where my eyes have been opened and I have seen angelic hosts, which were just as real as the people I come into contact with every day. These were seen with my eyes open and while being awake.

There have been other times where I have had visions in which I have seen things in the natural world in which we live, things that would be impossible to witness without a supernatural encounter. For instance, I have had visions in which I have seen secret meetings on the other side of the world and seen who was present and what was being said in those meetings. This should not be strange; these types of experiences should be normal for us, the people of God.

NORMAL CHRISTIANITY

I know that some people have a hard time with this type of experience. But we can see examples of this gift throughout Scripture, in both the Old Testament and the New. The gift of the seer can be seen in the example of Jesus "seeing" Nathaniel before He actually ever saw him. Jesus was explaining in a simple format that He had seen Nathaniel earlier in a vision. John tells us:

> The following day Jesus wanted to go to Galilee, and He found Philip and said to him, "Follow Me." Now Philip was from Bethsaida, the city of Andrew and Peter. Philip found Nathanael and said to him, "We have found Him of whom Moses in the law, and also the prophets, wrote—Jesus of Nazareth, the son of Joseph."
>
> And Nathanael said to him, "Can anything good come out of Nazareth?"
>
> Philip said to him, "Come and see."
>
> Jesus saw Nathanael coming toward Him, and said of him, "Behold, an Israelite indeed, in whom is no deceit!"
>
> Nathanael said to Him, "How do You know me?"
>
> Jesus answered and said to him, "Before Philip called you, when you were under the fig tree, I saw you."
>
> Nathanael answered and said to Him, "Rabbi, You are the Son of God! You are the King of Israel!"
>
> Jesus answered and said to him, "Because I said to you, 'I saw you under the fig tree,' do you believe? You will see greater things than these." And He said to him, "Most

assuredly, I say to you, hereafter you shall see heaven open,
and the angels of God ascending and descending upon the
Son of Man."

Jesus said sometime later, "Most assuredly, I say to you, the Son can do nothing of Himself, but what He sees the Father do; for whatever He does, the Son also does in like manner. For the Father loves the Son, and shows Him all things that He Himself does; and He will show Him greater works than these, that you may marvel" (John 5:19-20).

And that is not the only example we have in the Bible of someone seeing in the spirit realm. We can also see other examples, like the one instance in Elisha the prophet's life.

Now the king of Syria was making war against Israel; and
he consulted with his servants, saying, "My camp will be
in such and such a place." And the man of God sent to the
king of Israel, saying, "Beware that you do not pass this
place, for the Syrians are coming down there." Then the
king of Israel sent someone to the place of which the man
of God had told him. Thus he warned him, and he was
watchful there, not just once or twice.

Therefore the heart of the king of Syria was greatly
troubled by this thing; and he called his servants and said
to them, "Will you not show me which of us is for the
king of Israel?"

And one of his servants said, "None, my lord, O
king; but Elisha, the prophet who is in Israel, tells the king
of Israel the words that you speak in your bedroom" (II
Kings 6:8-12).

Elisha was operating exactly as a prophet should, as a watchman on the wall. He was having prophetic visions and encounters, observing the strategies and plans of the enemy king coming against the people of God. He then warned the king of Israel about this.

Many times the prophetic has opened up visions and shown me plans and even conversations taking place of which the Lord wanted me to be aware. This is a higher level of operation in the prophetic and it is released to those who can be trusted by the Lord in wisdom and discretion. Wouldn't it be amazing to avert a crisis or catastrophe by hearing such plans and warning the right person or people? God is calling all of us to grow in our prophetic gifts so that we can operate in this important "watchman on the wall" gift.

When Paul was trying to preach the gospel, he was sometimes hindered from going into certain areas. Upon one of these occasions, Paul had a vision in the night that changed his plans and drew him into a new direction. Luke tells us:

> And a vision appeared to Paul in the night. A man of Macedonia stood and pleaded with him, saying, "Come over to Macedonia and help us." Now after he had seen the vision, immediately we sought to go to Macedonia, concluding that the Lord had called us to preach the gospel to them (Acts 16:9-10).

Isn't it amazing how this gift can really convey clear messages, warnings, and instructions from the heavenly realm right into our hands? It is such a powerful thing when people pursue access to visions from God—what a blessing it is to the body of Christ. God not only gives us wisdom, but He can also give us direction for the spread of the gospel.

One example I find amazing and beautiful is the vision Stephen had outside the city walls as he was stoned to death. It was so beautiful that, as the world's system was killing this friend of God, he was caught up in a moment of awe and wonder, looking into the eyes of God and the heavenly city. In his act of selflessness, his natural eyes were opened and he saw heaven opened, and Jesus standing at the right hand of the Father. Luke again tells of this event:

> When they heard these things they were cut to the heart, and they gnashed at him with their teeth. But he, being full of the Holy Spirit, gazed into heaven and saw the glory of God, and Jesus standing at the right hand of God, and said, "Look! I see the heavens opened and the Son of Man standing at the right hand of God!"
>
> Then they cried out with a loud voice, stopped their ears, and ran at him with one accord; and they cast him out of the city and stoned him. And the witnesses laid down their clothes at the feet of a young man named Saul. And they stoned Stephen as he was calling on God and saying, "Lord Jesus, receive my spirit." Then he knelt down and cried out with a loud voice, "Lord, do not charge them with this sin." And when he had said this, he fell asleep. (Acts 7:54–60)

The seer gift is a gift in which a person's natural eyes see into the spirit world or into a situation that God wants to reveal to that person. In these moments, it becomes apparent how temporal earth and our human bodies are and how eternal God's world truly is.

CALLED TO BE YOU

The seer gift works at times a bit like watching a movie or TV screen. Often when I close my eyes and begin to allow the Spirit of God to fall on me, I will look past the blackness of having my eyes shut and images or a scene will appear as I watch. These images can be still like pictures, or they can be like movies. Obviously this must always go hand in hand with testing whether or not it is God showing me these things. This is a natural gift for some people, while others need to "pursue it" a little more. But always remember to never compare yourself to someone else's gift—you're called to be you, not them.

I used to hear other people's visionary experiences and it drove me to hunger after them too. It wasn't jealousy or competition I was experiencing, but a genuine hunger for all that God had for me. We can have as much of God as we want if we will just demonstrate genuine hunger and devotion to Him. Just like with hearing God's voice, our desire for seeing into the spirit realm can start small, like a mustard seed, and then grow into something amazing. I wanted to not only hear His voice but to see as well. So I embarked on a period of seeking God and fasting. I was totally resolved that I would see in the spirit realm.

I would often get in the car with some friends, and then we would drive around the city for an hour or two and pray over the city. A few months had gone by, and we had just finished praying and drove back into my friend's driveway, where we got out of the car.

All of a sudden I looked up at the house and I could see what looked like small spheres of different fiery colors flying in random paths all around the house, like a swarm of bees. I rubbed my eyes because I thought I was having a blood rush after standing up too quickly from being in a car for so long. I told my friend what I was seeing, and he looked up and saw them too! I knew I was looking at angels.

There were five dark spheres being chased away across the sky by a few of the fiery ones. We had been praying protection over that friend's home and family on that particular drive, and it was apparent that the demons that had been bothering him were being evicted as a result. I was in a state of awe as we both stared at these beings.

I lifted my hands and started thanking the Lord because my prayers were being answered. I was touched that He had given me my heart's request. I was crying as I thanked Him because it meant so much to me. And immediately, my eyes began to see even more! God later told me that as a result of my thankfulness, I was able to see more. I saw a sixty-foot-tall guardian angel standing on the front patio towering above me, kind of like Paul described, "seeing through a glass darkly" (1 Corinthians 13:12)—it was like looking through a slightly misted glass. I could see its form but not every detail of its being. He was holding a sword the size of a lamppost and he stood facing the north, an incredibly powerful being. As soon as I saw this angel, my physical body was pushed back into the hedge along the side of the driveway, which was about eight to ten feet back. This angel carried the presence of the Lord in such a powerful way that the glory pushed me back. The Lord later told me that His angels are always in His presence in heaven, and so when they come to earth they are covered in His glory and presence.

As this was happening, I saw a huge sphere that was about fifteen feet in diameter made of bright opaque light flying through his neighbor's backyard, and immediately when I saw it I recognized him as a sentry angel, patrolling the perimeter of the property. This one was moving with purpose and great momentum like a meteor. It was a truly powerful experience where God opened my eyes to see into the spirit realm.

I have seen angels in a bodily form, and I have also seen forms like these spheres described above. Maybe this is something different for you, but don't forget we are talking about another world here. In God's world there are beings who go before God and who have multiple faces and wings; there are beings with wheels inside wheels. We must not be so lost in our small mind-sets that we dismiss the world God lives in because it does not fit in with our imaginations or expectations.

This is why God said, "Eye has not seen, nor ear heard, nor have entered into the heart of man the things which God has prepared for those who love Him" (1 Corinthians 2:9). Heaven and the spirit world are so far-fetched from the landscape we have based our entire world around. The most ridiculous science-fiction movies and stories have not even come close to the realities of heaven. I had this experience with my eyes open, totally conscious of my earthly surroundings while seeing the spirit realm at the same time.

OPEN MY EYES, LORD

There was a period in my life when I could hear from God but had not yet seen open visions. Even as a young boy, for many years I had dreams from God into the spirit realm without realizing it, but I had not experienced visions while I was consciously awake. And so I became insatiably hungry for these types of visions. I remember making it the cry of my life, asking God for it daily and fasting over a period of six months, that God would open my eyes to see into the spirit realm. Then I began to see what God was showing me with my eyes opened. This is similar to what took place in 2 Kings 6.

While the king of Syria was making war against the people of Israel, Elisha heard what the king of Syria was planning, and so Elisha would let the king of Israel know so that they could be prepared. When the king of Syria heard about was happening, he sent men to Dothan to capture Elisha. "Therefore [the king of Syria] sent horses and chariots and a great army there, and they came by night and surrounded the city. And when the servant of the man of God arose early and went out, there was an army, surrounding the city with horses and chariots. And his servant said to him, 'Alas, my master! What shall we do?'" (2 Kings 6:14–15).

Elisha answered the servant and said, 'Do not fear, for those who are with us are more than those who are with them.' And Elisha prayed, and said, 'LORD, I pray, open his eyes that he may see.' Then the LORD opened the eyes of the young man, and he saw. And behold, the mountain was full of horses and chariots of fire all around Elisha" (2 Kings 6:16–17). God opened his eyes to see into the spirit realm, and the heavenly host that surrounded them was far greater than the army they could see with their natural eyes.

If you do not operate in this gift, then I would encourage you to build a relationship with someone who operates in it and ask them to lay hands on you and ask the Lord to impart the gift of seeing into your life, much like Elisha did with his servant. God longs for us to see into His heavenly realm, even more than we desire it.

For some people, seeing into the spirit realm comes easily, while for others it is a process. Seeing is actually having our real eyes opened to the reality of the spirit realm and what God wants us to see in the moment. What we see may be past, present, or future; it may be seeing the kingdom of heaven or the realm of hell. God shows us what is happening in the satanic realm at times to reveal the enemy's tactics and plans so that we can warn, pray, and position ourselves against his evil schemes.

The Father always wants to show us His goodness and reveal His plans toward us if we just give Him the opportunity to do so. Having the opportunity to look into His thoughts and plans toward us only gives us a better ability to agree and position ourselves with His dream over us.

BEWARE OF CONTAMINATION

The seeing gift is such an amazing gift, but it is also sensitive to contamination. Guarding your visible eye-gate so that your seeing eyes don't become dim is important. I grew up in New Zealand, and one of my great passions was hunting big game. I often used rifles with telescopic sights that had crosshairs to target the game animals from long distances. While hunting, I tried to keep any debris from getting into my rifle's barrel and to keep the mechanism of the weapon clean so it would function without a hitch when the opportunity came.

Just as important was my scope. I spent hours at the rifle range adjusting my scope while firing multiple bullets at targets from various distances, making sure it was just right. Once this was done, my gun was accurate when hunting. I had to be careful, however, that the gun was not jarred, as a slight bump could affect the accuracy of the scope by causing it to move fractionally out of alignment with the barrel of the weapon. I also needed to keep the lens of my scope clean. If grease, soil, or debris were smeared on the lens, then it could impair my vision at a crucial time of the hunt.

This is the best way I can describe the eye-gate of the prophetic person. It is like a person who hones one's senses over long periods of time in his or her walk with God and learns to become accurate in everything he or she says or does. That ability and accuracy needs to be guarded, protected, and treated with sober respect. The eye-gate is the scope for the prophet, making sure prophetic words are accurate and on target.

There are not many people who give much thought to protecting this gateway. A prophet must take great care not to pollute his or her eye-gate. For instance, watching certain movies or TV shows will allow certain traffic into your mind that may in itself not be sinful, but it may taint the clarity of your ability to see clearly. Likewise, any strongholds of sin will fog your ability to obtain concise vision from God. Lust is a major pollution to the clear wellspring of your spirit. If you allow pollution to enter your eyes, then your thinking or heart will become distorted. Just because you have a gift does not guarantee accuracy every time, especially if you are dabbling with sin or distraction.

Once I knew a man who had a strong prophetic gift but got involved in adultery. That same man, just days afterward, tried to prophesy over me. I immediately dismissed his words, as they had been tainted and I couldn't trust the integrity of the prophetic flowing through him. If someone is involved in perversion, then they will not be looking through a clear looking glass into the spirit. It will be tainted and unsafe. The Word of God clearly says that we are to guard our hearts above all else, for out of it flow the issues of life (Proverbs 4:23). I would encourage you to see this Scripture through the prophetic gift and you will understand the huge value of guarding your eye-gate.

STEWARDING VISIONS

As you grow in this ability to see, and you learn to steward visions at a personal level, then God will increase your realm of responsibility to that of the local church. And as you learn to steward your responsibility to the local church, then God may even increase your responsibility to national and global matters.

One night when praying over the city in which I lived at the time, I saw a vision of an incredibly tall being that was dressed in a long flowing white robe that looked similar to what Catholic priests wear. This being was over five hundred feet tall, and towered over the harbor and the central business district skyscrapers. It looked holy and spiritual with its religious-type clothing. He had his hands cupped around both sides of his mouth, in the same way people do when they are shouting over a distance to someone else. I could see words and sentences coming out of his mouth, being broadcasted over the entire city to the various areas all at once.

At face value someone might think this was God or an angel speaking over the city. But we are living in the times where we must partner with the Holy Spirit and ask Him what He is showing us in that moment. So I asked the Lord, and He told me that this was a ruling demonic principality in that territory. It was constantly speaking tradition, religion, and control. This spirit was a stronghold in this city and had been dictating mind-sets and belief systems made to look like culture and social traditions. It was not aimed purely at the church—it was targeting secular society, too.

When the Spirit of God shows us things like this, it is never for our entertainment or so we can have a science-fiction experience. It's always so we can be made aware of the realities in the unseen world that are present around us. God reveals these things so we can be aware of the plans, tactics, strongholds, and nature of our enemy. And once we are aware, we can then begin to pray against the enemy's strongholds and plans, and see the kingdom of heaven advance!

God longs to impart to you the seer gift. Are you desperate for it? Are you crying out for God to open your eyes to see into the supernatural realm?

CHAPTER 8

THE HEARING EAR

Most people want to know how to hear the voice of God. Hearing the voice of God usually doesn't come audibly through the natural ear, although it can. In most cases, however, I have found that the sensitive internal ear of the heart and spirit will hear the still small whisper of the Spirit of God. As a prophet or prophetic person, you will need to open and protect communications with the heart and Spirit of God so that you can hear Him clearly when He speaks.

This starts with the way you position yourself. James instructs us, "Draw near to God and He will draw near to you ..." (James 4:8). Walking in a state of humility and reverence before the Lord will cause His favor to increase on your life, and He will be drawn to you as a result. In drawing near to Him, you will hear His voice in a greater measure than you ever have before. It was precisely at this position where the Lord found meek and humble Samuel serving the Lord in the Temple. If we can prepare the runway of our hearts for the Spirit of God to land on, then He *will* speak!

Hearing God's voice did not come naturally or easily for me. My story began with an overwhelming hunger and an incessant and relentless desire to hear His voice at the age of twenty-three. This came after seeing the destructive power of man-made laws in church. I saw, like in the Dark Ages, that the "ministers" of the church had mostly bound up access to intimacy with God's voice, as they placed themselves on infallible platforms that were unattainable. Because perfection is impossible for humanity, it should never be portrayed by any of us. It was a terrible case of the blind leading the blind. These ministers would then dictate the portrayal of God's voice instead of encouraging their congregations to seek intimacy with Him through time spent in His presence and knowing the Word of God.

I want to make something very clear here: Without constantly reading the Word of God—the Bible—you will not recognize His voice when He speaks. I have seen much destruction of "God said" statements being made in churches, families, and even in businesses—I became intolerant to it unless I knew it was one hundred percent authentic. This drove me on a quest to find and become acquainted with the legitimate voice of God. My intent was not to avoid making errors in my life by listening to people who claimed "God said" or by listening to any random thought in my mind and labeling it as coming from God! It is impossible to never make an error in hearing God, but it's important not to play a game of russian roulette in pursuit of hearing His direction either.

Even though I had prophetic dreams in my younger years, I did not always hear God's voice clearly or consistently. Around the age of twenty-three, however, I spent about six months praying and fasting to hear God's voice in more of a consistent and intimate way. I was determined to hear His voice clearly, and I would not settle for anything less. And so I began to hear His voice after that six-month period, and, just like a child, it started with one word at a time. His presence would always descend on me to confirm His voice. Since that time, I have learned to double and triple check each time to make sure it is He who is speaking to me.

In time, God began to speak sentences and tell me things more descriptively, and I was able to recognize His voice all the more. Over the years of interacting with the voice of God, I have been able to differentiate between the voices of Jesus, the Father, and the person of the Holy Spirit. Understanding the difference between who is speaking at any given moment actually brings a clearer understanding of what God is saying.

There are times when recognizing which person of the Godhead is speaking brings greater clarity to the heart of God in these moments. When I heard the Father speak to me recently, it carried so much more weight as it conveyed the Father's heart and affirmation into the area I was walking. He said, "Andrew, son, I am with you in this next season you are entering, and I will cause the blessing to flourish on you like never before." Coming from the Father, and having His affirmation and presence with me in the next season, carries a huge weight and comfort with it. It was not only comforting to me but also empowering and encouraging. I am not taking away from the Holy Spirit's or Jesus's voice, but for each specific situation God chooses the best person of the Godhead to speak for that moment.

Learn to hear God's voice and your world will be changed when you do! It only takes hearing God's leading on a few occasions to understand that unforeseen calamity can be avoided, immeasurable blessing can be encountered, and God's perfect will can be followed into the way and path of peace and heavenly abundant provision.

You have a right to hear the voice of God! The Scriptures declare, " Yet they will by no means follow a stranger, but will flee from him, for they do not know the voice of strangers" (John 10:5). Hearing the voice of God goes beyond your right and it becomes your duty to connect with your heavenly Father's voice. Listening to His voice will cause you to walk in the way of life, and life more abundantly, according to His plans and thoughts. And it will also direct your path away from the snares and traps of the enemy, who desires to slow you down.

DROWNING OUT DISTRACTIONS

How do we hear God's voice in the midst of all the noise of life, whispers of the enemy, and our own thoughts? The Bible says, "Be still, and know that I am God ..." (Psalm 46:10). We will never hear His voice if we do not allow a stillness to come into our hearts, which positions us to hear Him.

Hearing God's voice comes from the practice of waiting on God. It is a learned familiarity and acquaintance with Him that sets apart those who hear His voice from those who do not. When you were a child, you became familiar unconsciously with your parents' voices because of repeatedly hearing them talk to you. When you heard the voice of a stranger, even if you could not see him or her, you would know that voice was not the voice of your parents. This is the way it is with God.

When you hear God's voice and allow repetition to take place over time, you will become tuned into hearing His voice and discerning His sound. This is important because, just like when Satan came to tempt Jesus on His forty-day fast in the desert, Satan will talk to you and try to imitate God's voice at times. Sometimes it will even sound scriptural and godly.

In 1 Samuel 3, God came to Samuel in the temple when he was a child. Eli's (who was the priest at the time) eyes had grown dim. I do not believe this reference has as much to do with his actual eyesight growing dim as much as his spiritual eyesight. Eli's sons were having sex with prostitutes on the temple steps, and they were taking far more than they were permitted to from the sacrifices on the altar. There was a flame in Eli that had long grown dim, and he allowed this to carry on without upholding the righteous standard of "holiness unto the Lord." And because that flame had grown dim on the inside, his clarity to hear God's voice had also diminished.

When Samuel heard someone call his name in the middle of the night, he went to Eli to see if he was the one who kept calling. Eli knew it was the Lord, and so he instructed the young boy to answer the Lord the next time God called. But the real tragedy here is that

God had to override the appointed high priest who should have been the intermediary between God and the people of Israel. Eli should have been God's first port-of-call when He needed to speak. Yet, because Eli had tolerated sin instead of confronting it, a part of his ability to receive and hear God became limited. We read how God selected Samuel and used him powerfully, and also how God brought judgment on the sinful sons of Eli.

Here is the point that every prophet and prophetess should take seriously: If sin is tolerated and a blind eye is turned, particularly in the prophet's life, that flame will slowly but surely become more and more quenched. And if you keep resisting the Holy Spirit in your heart, then God will eventually speak to another and bypass you. We must walk before God soberly and with all reverence. The Word of God states in Psalm 111:10, "The fear of the LORD is the beginning of all wisdom ..." Wisdom is a Spirit, and you will not have access to Him unless you walk in the fear, holiness, and righteousness of the Lord. If you want to have an ear that is attuned to the voice of God, then you must drown out all distractions and stay pure in heart and life.

CHAPTER 9

THE SENSORY GIFT

Did you know that the cliché statement "I feel that" actually began in the church? It came out of the Pentecostal and charismatic denominations, and it was spoken when the Holy Spirit would move so much that everyone would "feel" His tangible presence flowing in the room. When it comes to us growing in the office of the prophet or in the prophetic gift, we need to desperately understand the sensory gift. What do I mean by sensory gift?

The sensory gift is actually your physical senses that experience the supernatural around you. Over the years the Holy Spirit has taught me to become more sensitive to these feelings. I personally think that as my spirit has grown in God and Christ has been formed inside of my being, I have become more acutely aware of my spiritual surroundings. This oftentimes comes in the form of a physical awareness of either angelic or demonic presences, and the various manifestations of God's presence taking place around me.

I was in a hotel in Singapore on a ministry trip when I felt a dark presence walk into the room. My spirit (not my mind) recognized the atmospheric presence in the room as a principality, and so I began to pray in tongues. My spirit and body physically recognized where the demonic principality was standing in the room, although I could not see it.

Then I sensed Jesus walk into the room. Although I could not see Him, I felt His presence as He walked right up next to my bed and put His hand over my heart. I could feel heat coming off His hands and into my body. He said, "Don't worry about this; I've got you covered," and then He began to laugh. Again, I couldn't hear Him with my physical ears, but my spirit heard Him. Right at that time, two powerful angels ran right through the door of my hotel room and tackled the principality like rugby or American football players would, and then they ran him right out the hotel window and down sixteen stories!

Another example of a time where I functioned in my sensory gift was in an extremely difficult situation where I had to find out the truth. There was a person in my church I was counseling about an unhealthy relationship he was hiding, and this person had made up his mind to proceed but was under a spell of his own emotions. I would ask him a question and he would look me straight in the eyes and give me what looked like a genuine answer that appeared to be honest and full of integrity. That is, until the Holy Spirit partnered with me in that meeting.

Every time this individual would lie to me, I would feel a heat wave rush over my body. It became like a thermometer where every time a lie was told I would know and challenge that person until he knew that God was in on this conversation and began to break toward honesty. And eventually he repented. I called this my Holy Spirit lie detector; it became something that I now often operate in.

It is such an amazing thing when the Holy Spirit partners with you in such a way that when everyone else sees truth, He shows you a lie. This is such an integral gift to the body of Christ—being able to see and know something that to the natural eye is unseen, is invaluable.

Another way this gift works is that you can sense God's activity and movement in a moment, in a situation, or in a room. Having the sensory awareness of when God's Spirit "jumps" in a room or an electrically charged atmosphere surrounds us when something is said straight from His heart, we begin to be able to draw that much closer to Him and flow with Him in His priorities.

Often I will tangibly feel God's presence in most circumstances when a genuine prophetic word is given, an anointed song is sung, or even when I verbalize a decision that God has advised me on. Our spirits and God's Spirit are designed to interact in the spirit realm even more than the natural world. On the opposite spectrum, there is an eerie and dark presence that can be physically sensed when the demonic is present as well. I have been awakened from a deep sleep at times to an overwhelming sense of darkness, and my natural response is to immediately pray in tongues until all of the demonic presence is replaced by God's presence and atmosphere.

The fact that the demonic can get into your home or bedroom is not a failure on your part; you are a threat to the kingdom of hell. However, at times these fallen angels will visit you to try and bring fear or torment to your heart. These demons can carry such a powerful evil presence that at times I have been unable to move. Never bow in fear, however; just pray in the Spirit until they leave. The Word of God says that we are to "resist the devil and he will flee from you" (James 4:7). The fact that you can feel this presence assists you in navigating the terrain of your life in the natural and the spiritual realms.

When you tangibly feel the presence of God, it is often a sign to stop and look into what He is trying to show you in that moment. I made many mistakes early on in my walk with the Holy Spirit by simply interpreting His presence as a confirmation that He was saying yes. But sometimes He was actually directing me to stop and investigate the details of what He was trying to say. For instance, "feeling" the anointing or presence of God can actually be a warning, not a confirmation. Never be hasty in your interpretation of what you feel God is showing you. Always take time and allow Him as much time as He wants to clarify His perfect will. This has often been the cliff leading to many falls in peoples' lives. Take your time to learn His leading.

Many people use goosebumps as a confirmation of God's approval. In many cases it can be, but not all of the time. The Bible says that we are to test the spirits, not be fooled by any old thing. I have watched Christians, and even myself in times past, make terrible decisions based on feeling the Holy Spirit goosebumps. It's important that when you feel something, you stop and double and triple check what the good and acceptable will of the Lord is in that specific situation. You see, the Word and the Spirit are one—the

Spirit will never disagree with the Word—and so your sensory gift is not going to contradict the Word of God. If it does, then you are wrong, for the Word of God will always be right.

There is a certain presence that emanates from angels that is different to the presence that is evident when God is in the room. They are similar but not totally the same. You see, angels are constantly in the presence of God as they continually come before the throne of God, so they bear the fragrance and mark of His presence. As I have grown in my walk with God, I have begun to differentiate between these.

The more you pursue God's presence and person, the more you will be familiar with His distinct traits. In time I became aware of the differences between the presence of Jesus as opposed to the Father or the Holy Spirit. It's like learning a new language—at first everything sounds similar and then in time each word takes on its own distinct meaning and context.

Being aware of God's presence helps me navigate my interactions with the spirit realm much better. It also helps me sense when an evil spirit is near. When you are accustomed to and sensitive to the presence of God, you become acutely aware of everything else. Have you ever been in a conversation or a situation when you have felt an eerie, dark, or just plain evil feeling? The demon of fear has a distinct signature on its presence—it is one of threat, dread, and terror. The world understands this feeling, and it is much more than an emotion; it is a spiritual entity identifying itself

Most people just write this off as an emotion or feeling, but it is actually their spirit reacting to the presence nearby. As sons and daughters of God, we must resist the devil and every demon from hell when they are present and they will flee. We are to bow to the King of heaven when He comes. You wouldn't want to be ignored when you walk into a room, right? So learn to become sensitive to the presence of God and His messengers, the angels. This gifting needs to be learned so that you're not fooled by cheap counterfeits.

Some of you reading this will recall the Scripture that says we walk by faith not by sight, and that faith is not about feelings. I'm not referring to emotional feelings here when we are talking about the prophetic gifts; I'm referring to a physical awareness of a spiritual reality.

You can see an example of this when two of the disciples walked with a man on the road to Emmaus. During their journey this man began to explain and open up the Scriptures in their conversation. As He did so, they began to feel a burning inside their spirits, as they sensed the presence of Jesus by His words. They did not realize till after the mystery man had departed, as they discussed and exchanged notes between themselves saying, "Did our hearts not burn within us?" (Luke 24:32). They had an inward burning that was confirming the presence of Jesus.

Like most of the gifts that God gives, this gift will be increased by being intimate with God and spending time in His presence. You begin to recognize tangible traits of His presence that are both physically sensed but also spiritually detected. It is both a practiced presence but also a tangible gift of discernment that you can feel many times in a sensory manifestation.

If this is not yet an area that you function in, then ask the Holy Spirit to teach you and cause you to flow in this gift. God will not withhold from you any good thing. But it is also important to not compare yourself with others who flow in this gift. Don't allow jealousy to eat at your heart; rather, talk to God about it. He is not partial to anyone, so you are just as much qualified for the gifts of God as the next person. So simply ask the Lord, for He won't withhold any good thing from you. Sometimes gifts can take a while to arrive, while other gifts can come sooner than later—but all gifts take time to develop.

CHAPTER 10

DISCERNING OF SPIRITS

When I was only three years old, there was a man walking around aimlessly whom my family and I would see all over town as we drove around the city. I did not really know anything about the Spirit of God; we were in a very conservative and non-charismatic church—and I was three! But something in me discerned that something wasn't right with that man, and before I knew anything about demonic spirits, I spoke up one day and said, "There's the wandering spirit." From that day on, that's how I referred to that man's state.

With toddlers and infants, and even young children, there can be such a purity of spirit where discernment is much more clear than in an adult. This is why it's so important to enter the kingdom, or approach our lives in the kingdom, like a little child. Jesus said, "Assuredly, I say to you, unless you are converted and become as little children, you will by no means enter the kingdom of heaven. Therefore whoever humbles himself as this little child is the greatest in the kingdom of heaven" (Matthew 18:3–4).

WHAT IS DISCERNING OF SPIRITS?

Our spirits recognize spirits of good and spirits of evil. Paul lists "discerning of spirits" as one of the nine gifts that Holy Spirit gives to His people in order to benefit the body of Christ and for the common good (1 Corinthians 12:10). To discern is to rightly divide or correctly judge a matter for what it is or isn't, and so discerning of spirits is the gift that simply recognizes the natures of various spiritual entities.

The devil wants to deal with immature and undiscerning Christians in the battlefield of life, for these people are easily fooled and misled. Do not be one of these shallow and gullible Christians; rather, make a decision today to take advice from Paul: "Study to shew thyself approved unto God, a workman that needeth not to be ashamed, rightly dividing the word of truth" (2 Timothy 2:15 KJV). This implies that wrongly dividing the word of truth could bring shame. The Word and the Spirit are one, and so investing in the Word will give you sharpness in the spirit realm. Testing the spirits involves seeing if a person or an angel acknowledges Jesus as the only Son of God, born of a virgin, died on a cross, conquered Satan, took the keys of sin and death, and rose victorious. Every person or angel that does not do this is not of the kingdom of heaven.

Discerning of spirits is not limited to angels and demons alone. People are influenced and given over to various spirits as well. Children of God are given to the Spirit of God and are led by His voice. At various times, some of the children of God will be influenced by spirits that are not of God, but that does not mean that they have turned from God and are now possessed by demons. Peter told Jesus that He would never go to the cross, and Jesus replied by saying, "Get behind me, Satan." Jesus was rebuking the spirit that was influencing Peter, and, in fact, was speaking through Peter. On another occasion, Jesus rebuked some of His disciples for offering to call down fire from heaven to consume people opposing Jesus. His reply was, "You do not know what spirit you are of" (Luke 9:55).

Christians can be given over to or have strongholds in certain areas of their lives. Just take fear as an example. There have been many occasions when others around me have made statements that are motivated by fear. Once those words left their lips, I felt the cold chill of the intimidation of a spirit press on my emotions and cause me to feel like backing down. But this is not faith, and my God is a Spirit of faith.

That feeling of fear, fright, or intimidation is often a spirit that is on assignment to attack us. We must learn to discern it. I am not taking away from wisdom-based advice here, but I am describing the eerie spirit that will try to terrify us and cause us to give up. In some cases, it can oppress people randomly, but others carry and are bound by this spirit as it tries to control the atmosphere around them. If this is you, then you need to get deliverance and cast out this demonic oppression from your life. If it is a brother or sister in the Lord, then pray for them and use discretion and wisdom to direct them to get deliverance. If it is a nonbeliever, then pray that they are saved and delivered from this bondage. But above all, do not submit to these spirits!

People who are not walking with God will yield to various spirits. If there is someone who has opened a door to a perverse or seductive spirit, when in proximity to that individual, I can feel the uncleanness of that spirit. Its agenda will be to somehow get my attention or to influence my thoughts. In this case I recognize it in action and begin to pray in tongues and declare that the assignment against me has no power, breaking the spirit's power in Jesus's name. Make sure you do this, and do not *ever* accept an atmosphere that is not from God.

You are called into the original blessing that God gave Adam when Adam first opened his eyes: "Be blessed, multiply, and have dominion." You are called to walk in dominion as a person who is made in the image of God! You walk in absolute authority above the atmosphere, not in it or below it. You, as a child of God and a coheir with Christ, are called to dictate the atmosphere of heaven into your environment and to multiply the kingdom into those around you. Learn to discern the nature and scent between the two realms in the spirit.

DISCERNING MUCH MORE

Discerning of spirits is not just the identification of spirits, whether demonic or godly, but it also applies to discerning the intents and motives of people in specific scenarios. The writer of

Hebrews said this: "For the word of God is living and powerful, and sharper than any two-edged sword, piercing even to the division of the soul and spirit, and joints and marrow, and is a discerner of the thoughts and intents of the heart" (Hebrew 4:12).

As you navigate through the various situations in your life and ministry, you will need to be able to discern not only certain spirits in operation in various areas and circumstances, but you will also need to be able to discern people's motives. There have been countless occasions in which a person or group of people have interacted with me and wanted me to do, say, or agree in a certain way. Everything seemed reasonable with the external environment, but I had a check inside my spirit. Sometimes, I do not have any reason for this alarm, but I have come to know this as the Holy Spirit's caution coupled with His gift of discernment.

Sometimes people are so good at selling an idea that it's hard to use the face value as your assessment. You have to learn to live walking in the Spirit so that you can discern these things. Sometimes their agenda or motives are so well hidden behind their apparent concern for your best interests that you will only detect these snares by operating in this gift of discerning. Having a sound grasp of the Word of God is a good plumb line to use against what people say. For instance, having a sound grasp on the book of Proverbs will teach you wisdom so that when someone speaks wisdom you will recognize it, and equally you will recognize foolishness.

Having the Word soundly invested into your life is a crucial part of walking in the prophetic realm, but it is not the entirety of the gift. You also need to learn the ways of the Holy Spirit, becoming intimate with Him so that when He is uncomfortable you become uncomfortable. When there is something hidden, then you begin to recognize it and perceive the intentions that are not physically obvious.

But discerning of spirits is not a sign of intelligence as in a mentally-grasped ability; it is a learned walk and an impartation from God to see and discern the unseen characteristics and plans of others so that you will not be caught unawares, which is crucial to anyone who is called to be a prophet.

Paul was in the markets and there was a slave girl with the spirit of divination speaking out the truth, that these men were servants of God who were showing the way of salvation. She was calling out information about them that she could not have naturally known. Either she was a God-fearing person who listened to the Holy Spirit, or this was a demonic counterfeit gift in operation. The truth of the matter is that most people probably thought it was really sweet and beautiful that this girl was declaring apparent truth.

The really notable thing here is that the slave girl was calling out a factual word of knowledge that was in all actuality the truth! But what was not apparent to almost everyone in those markets was that the girl was speaking facts inspired by demonic entities. Paul had a strong gift of discerning of spirits that he had developed over time in his personal walk with God and his knowledge of the Word of God.

In many churches today, that girl would have been given the microphone and asked to minister. But Paul walked in the Spirit and saw through the façade of empowered knowledge in the girl, and called it what it was—a demon. It was from that place that he was able to identify the real operation going on in her life. He proceeded to cast the demon out of her that was enabling this apparent prophetic gift, which was really demonic in nature.

TWO MAIN SOURCES

Discerning of spirits comes from two main sources: One is a solid grasp of and investment in the Word of God into our lives, and the second is a relationship with the person of the Holy Spirit in which we learn to become sensitive to His sometimes softly announced presence. We are called to be good stewards of His person, to the point that we start to protect His feelings and honor His preferences and His sensitivities.

We feel His pleasure when things are being said and taking place that are honoring His Spirit. Then, when things begin happening or being said that are not from God, this grieves the Spirit, giving us an alarming feeling that triggers in our spirits. As time has gone on in my walk with the Holy Spirit, I have felt my heart, spirit, and even feelings merge with God's agenda where His priorities and feelings start to look like my own. His presence becomes such a valuable and precious thing in our lives that we would rather risk offending other people that offending Him.

In the same way, as this relationship grows and Christ is formed in you, you will also begin to sense when certain things being said are of right motive or wrong and whether things are being influenced by an angelic entity or a demonic one. You'll also be able to discern when the various manifestations of the Spirit of God become apparent in a particular place. For instance, God has many names in the Scriptures, and each name represents a characteristic or nature of God's person. With each one of those names of God, we can see and experience the Spirit of God manifest as a presence that enters a room, and in each case there is the same Spirit. But as you walk with God and grow in intimacy, you will begin to differentiate distinct differences and attributes of the various facets of the person of God.

An illustration of this would be the fear of the Lord. When the fear of the Lord enters a place, there comes more than just an intellectual sense of soberness. There comes an ambiance of tangible fear, respect, and reverence of the Lord that can be experienced by each person present. It is like the whole atmosphere of a room will change when God presents Himself in a certain way.

Learning to discern what He is doing or what facet of His nature He is choosing to show Himself in a given situation is so important for any son or daughter of God to be aware of, especially a prophet. Moses asked God to reveal Himself in His glory, but God chose to present Himself in His goodness. This is not a case of God having a multiple personality disorder; this is a case of God being far more complex than we could ever comprehend, so He has chosen to present Himself to us in faceted traits of His amazing and rich personality.

We are invited to partner with the Holy Spirit to become discerning of God's various and multitiered nature so we can best partner with Him in what He is doing in each and every situation. Daniel said, "The people that do *know* their God shall be strong, and do exploits" (Daniel 11:32 KJV). May our hunger and desire for the discerning of spirits grow more and more.

CHAPTER 11

THE PROPHETIC IS A PORTAL

The prophetic as a portal may be a difficult thought for some people to grasp, but please know that God's creativity and ways are so much bigger than and outside the parameters of the world we know as normal in our day-to-day lives. The act of prophecy is like opening a glimpse into the thoughts and plans of another world. When God gives us a message for someone else, it is an opening up of the spiritual world of heaven in which a message travels through a portal to our natural environment.

Prophecy really is the world of God's heart. It is the expressed heart of God in a matter. And hearing it causes us to see a glimpse of His heart in each situation. But God lives in heaven and here we are on the earth, so the portal is like a spiritual doorway through which a message or vision crosses over from God's world into ours. It can also be the doorway through which God invites us to come and see into His world. A perfect example of this is in Revelation. John writes:

*After these things I looked, and behold, a door standing
open in heaven. And the first voice which I heard was like
a trumpet speaking with me, saying, "Come up here, and I
will show you things which must take place after this."*

*Immediately I was in the Spirit; and behold, a throne
set in heaven, and One sat on the throne. (Revelation 4:1-2)*

The message that comes into our world from His is available for
all who hear and believe the word!

Star Trek was one of America's most famous sci-fi TV series
in the past few decades. Did you ever hear the catchphrase from
the show, "Beam me up, Scotty"? A look at this is helpful in order
to understand an aspect of the power of the prophetic as a portal.
A transporter would dematerialize people from one place and
rematerialize them either to a specific destination or back to the
Starship Enterprise. The prophetic is like a transporter portal in the
sense that we are able to see into the plans and purposes of God.
I'm not saying this is a literal example, although there are examples
of this type of experience actually happening, like when Philip was
translated in Acts 8:39–40.

Think of this portal as an opening between worlds, in which you
can hear the voice of God speaking over you. The doorway of this
portal is usually a prophet who speaks the word of the Lord, or a vision
that comes to a person. It can be a window through which provisions,
promises, empowerments, and blessings are directly delivered from
heaven into our lives and world, but it can also be the opening of a
gateway into a whole new dimension by being transported to and
seeing into the realities of God's thoughts and plans.

Let's look at the portal that opened up when Jesus died and the veil in the temple was torn open, forever making a way into the Holy of Holies (Matthew 27:51).

JESUS'S DEATH OPENED A PORTAL

Jesus's death caused so much of God's power to be released into the world that some of the dead people buried in Jerusalem actually came alive and started walking around the city! The moment Jesus died, something happened that rippled a portal between the spirit realm and the natural one.

The veil in the temple that separated the inner court from the Holy of Holies was four inches thick! Have you ever seen a curtain that thick? It was said that the material of the curtain and the way it was fabricated made it so strong that horses tied to opposing sides could not tear it apart! And yet the moment Jesus died, there was a huge earthquake and the veil was torn, which was a prophetic sign that got everyone's attention. To make the sign even more vividly graphic, something happened that caused people to be raised from the dead! More people were raised from the dead in Jesus's death than during His life.

The cause of these events—the earthquake, the tearing of the veil, and the dead being raised—was the result of a portal that opened up between God's realm and ours through what Jesus did on the cross! There was a shaking, there was access and freedom into the sacred and holy places of God, and then there was resurrection power released. The tearing of the veil released the reality of heaven into earth, the dead were raised as life-giving power flowed, and access was granted into the Holy of Holies in the temple as liberty came with the new covenant.

Jesus is the way. He made access to the Father, but also into His power. The prophetic is one of the keys that can open doorways and portals in the spirit realm and alter the course of this natural world.

There was also a portal that Jesus opened in the garden of Gethsemane. Jesus spent time with the Father, so much so that when He responded to the soldiers who came to arrest Him, when He told them, "I am He," that very statement was so potent in its essence that it knocked the guards backward to the ground. The authority He walked in opened the realms of the glory of God; heaven was opened and it struck the soldiers with such power that they all fell to the ground.

As prophets, we must allow time and intimacy with the Father to build in such a way that when we speak on behalf of God, there is a prophetic portal opened up into the heavenlies, and the manifested power and anointing of God is released!

RECEIVING WORDS MEANT FOR OTHERS

Have you ever heard another person getting a prophetic word and felt like you would really like that same word spoken over you? Well, it often can be! Some words are extremely specific to certain people or territories, and these words are generally exclusive. But many words that are delivered create what I like to describe as an opening into the heavenly realms when spoken. It is almost as if a portal or doorway opens when the prophetic starts to flow. And in moments like these, you can catch certain words and claim them for yourself, too.

Here is the key to being able to receive other words being spoken for others: If a prophetic word is being brought forth for another person about walking into a season of breakthrough in his or her life, or perhaps in a specific area like in a relationship or breakthrough in his or her finances, that word opens up a portal in the spirit realm. There is an empowerment from God for what is being released. God, who is the Spirit of prophecy, is fueling what is being spoken about to flow from His world into this one.

Another word for this empowerment is anointing. When that specific prophetic anointing is flowing for the specific area that you need or desire, then it is time that you put your hands up to heaven and reach into that realm and tell the Father, "I claim that word for my life too!"

It is like the healing pools that were built around Jerusalem (John 5:1–15). It was at these pools that when the angel of the Lord stirred the waters, the first person who entered into the water was made well. It wasn't the water that made the person well—the water wasn't magical. It was only the portal and realm that was opened up between the throne of God and the peoples' needs. The first person into that pool would be healed because they accessed more than water or an angel's presence—they accessed realms of heaven coming to the earth. The prophetic is much the same. It is a moment of access that can be either agreed with or not valued, becoming a claimed or missed opportunity.

The amazing thing about the prophetic, now that we are living in this New Covenant with the veil torn and access directly to the Father, is that it is not just for the first person into the pool anymore! It's for all. You can piggyback on to another person's prophetic word when you partner your faith with what is spoken because you are agreeing with the Spirit of God, not just dead law. You're not stealing another person's word—it's one hundred percent for them—but you can claim all or part of that for you, too! There is no competition in the kingdom of God when we all stand in our own true identities in Christ.

The prophetic can be like a school of tuna swimming through the ocean past a fleet of fishing boats—any boats that have their nets out are likely to catch tuna! If not, then they won't catch anything. For instance, I have heard prophetic words that were clearly from God to consider a certain natural mineral as an investment on the stock market because God would take that obscure mineral stock and would bless it. This doesn't sound spiritual, does it? Well, God told Adam about the eastern river, and that down that river was where the gold was good! It is a similar principle. Never limit God's ability to flow into all corners of life with His prophetic mouthpieces!

This word was given to a few people regarding investment in the stock; however, a few others heard this word also, prayed over it, and invested in it too. Time passed and the stock grew in value.

And they reaped the harvest when the word came to pass, just as the prophet had said. This is a good example of someone claiming a prophetic word and getting a piece of the action.

BURYING OUR TALENTS

I have even seen situations in which the word of the Lord was released over someone's life and they belittled, devalued, or disdained the prophetic, but someone else in the room didn't. In this situation I witnessed the outworking of part of the parable that Jesus told in Matthew 25:14–30, concerning the talents. There was one of the three servants who devalued his talent using the excuse of fear, and so he buried his talent instead of investing it. This servant's talent was stripped from him and given to another who took the opportunity to work with his master's estate.

Isaiah declared, "So shall My word be that goes forth from My mouth; it shall not return to Me void, but it shall accomplish what I please, and it shall prosper *in the thing* for which I sent it" (Isaiah 55:11). God is always overseeing His word to ensure that nothing He says ever falls to the ground.

I am discovering that the most sacred thing that God has is His own Word. The more I look into this, and the more I consider Scriptures like the parable of the talents, the more I see that when prophecies are discarded by people, a transfer is already underway. There is no way to engineer a transfer of a promise. If you position yourself toward God's prophetic word of honor, there is a good chance you may walk into it. There have been certain times when a person has discarded or become disqualified to walk into the promised word, while another person is anointed by the Lord, sometimes knowingly and other times without realizing what is taking place. There have been many times men and women were called to walk alongside certain ministers, and the prophecies over the ministers fell onto the people who were walking alongside of them. We can see this with God anointing David to be king of Israel, after having rejected Saul's heart who was still on the physical throne (1 Samuel 15:26).

I am astounded as I recall, over the course of time, these same people give up and walk away from their positions. And I have marveled as I have witnessed the unspoken transfer of the role and the destiny carried in the original prophetic promise over to the other person who is positioned correctly and willing to step into such a role and promise. The conclusion I am coming to is that God will achieve the fullness of His word independently of the individual's obedience.

When the king sits on the throne, he is fulfilling his life's purpose. But if for any reason he abdicates or steps down from his rule, then another successor will be chosen and appointed. This is the case for the word of the Lord. It shall not return void, but it shall return (to the Lord), having achieved what it was sent to do. When God releases His word out of an opening from His world to ours, regardless of individual's agreement, His word will remain valid and transfer until it rests on someone who is willing to agree and accomplish what it was sent to do.

Be aware that there is always going to be someone who values what God is saying through the doorways opening from heaven. If the person originally intended to carry the word of the Lord devalues it, then God will always have someone else waiting to pick it up. Recognize prophetic portals when they open over your life. Value them. Catch what God is releasing.

When the children of Israel arrived at the Jordan River the first time, they failed to believe God's promises due to the ten spies who feared, lied, and issued a false report. God's word did not return to him void. It was simply transferred to the following generation, and forty years later His promise was proved true and Joshua led Israel into the land God promised Abram.

Never allow yourself to be a person who grows weary and turns back from the plow of your journey toward the promises of God, and specifically in the things of prophetic promise. It will cost you to stand in your field of promise. Don't let it be said of your life that you sold your prophetic birthright for an easier path. There is always a Jacob willing to take the blessing from a dismissive Esau; there's always an Esther who is positioned to replace a Vashti. Queen Vashti was replaced by Esther because of her refusal to honor the King (Esther 1).

When someone disregards a word from God, he or she neglects or buries his or her talent. That word is still valid because God breathed it out. It will continue looking for someone or many to partner with the word, to stand up and say, "Here I am, Lord. Send me." I have seen callings, prophecies, and even mantles transfer from one person to another simply because someone would not pick up and engage with the prophetic word or call.

STEWARDING PORTALS FROM HEAVEN

Portals open up new doorways and opportunities, but we must be faithful to steward and value the prophetic that comes through these moments to ensure the vision God has over our lives is fulfilled in these areas. There was a time in my own life when I was about twenty-nine in which I had held to a word that God had spoken to me personally, and it cost me everything to hold onto it. I had made some weighty personal sacrifices to be obedient to God's word.

Shortly after that time, I was alone in the middle of the night in a national park where I would often go to seek the Lord. Unexpectedly a whirlwind made of light descended over my body, spinning around me, like a cocoon. I could barely stand ... I could feel the beautiful presence of God all over me. As I stood there taking it in, God spoke to me: "Thank you for doing what I said. Because you have been obedient and not compromised, I will now increase your prophetic anointing to greater levels—you will notice it from now on." After that moment of prophetic visitation, my life was changed and the prophetic gift on my life went to new levels of authority and accuracy.

Obedience and faithfulness entice visitations from the Lord. These moments, where the heavens open and prophetic words are released over your life, are absolutely life-changing and invaluable. The prophetic is a portal into the heavenly realm, allowing God's world and word to visit ours. It is through these portals that Jesus's prayer is answered: "Your kingdom come. Your will be done on earth as it is in heaven" (Matthew 6:10).

CHAPTER 12

PROPHETIC DECLARATIONS AND DECREES

There are different forms of prophetic utterances or announcements, which I separate into two different categories, declarations and decrees. To understand the differences between these two categories, let's look a little closer at each of them. Often it can be unclear as to which of these two a particular prophetic word can fall into, so let's outline a few hallmarks so you will grasp the contrast between prophetic declarations and decrees.

First, we need a word of caution. One of the greatest principles we will need to master as a student of the prophetic is the potency of our tongue and the control of it. James 3:2–12 reminds us that the tongue is very powerful and can be an instrument of life-giving power or a tool of death. And Jesus instructs us, "A good man out of the good treasure of his heart brings forth good; and an evil man out of the evil treasure of his heart brings forth evil. For out of the abundance of the heart his mouth speaks" (Luke 6:45).

This is actually a matter-of-the-heart condition. This is because we cannot authentically declare or decree from a heart that is not full of good treasure. We must personally and regularly encounter the love of the Father so that we communicate everything He says through His heart for His people.

A PROPHETIC DECLARATION

A prophetic declaration is an official announcement of something commencing, coming, or something that is present. It is a formal or explicit statement. It carries with it elements of fighting, hope, and preparation. It also carries with it a lot of faith. To declare or announce something is to set out plainly the truth or to shout out a statement.

In a troubled world where situations can appear dark and daunting, the voice of declaration carves the path and destination to your future. The Bible says, "Death and life are in the power of the tongue, and those who love it will eat its fruit" (Proverbs 18:21). I referred to the fact that God our Father created everything for Adam with His voice; He breathed into the clay that His hands fashioned and Adam became a living being. With His words, God spoke into being *everything* that we know to be creation. If we have been made in His image and likeness, then the power of His creative prophetic utterance is also on our tongues as well. This is where we must learn to become extremely careful and watchful over our words.

When we are in a bad situation, we really have two choices: we can speak into our situation negative words that cause death, or we can declare life and hope that brings the answer! The choice is simple to admit, but much more difficult to practice. It's the discipline of stopping yourself from speaking negativity and words of death over yourself, your life, your situation, your future, or anyone and anything else around you. Don't be fooled, for whatever you sow you will also reap.

For example, if you said, "I'll never get out of this financial mess," versus "In Jesus's name, I speak every debt to be paid and cleared over my life." This is a declaration. Then you can take it further and decree like a king or queen, because that is what you are as God's son or daughter. To declare is to speak something that isn't into being. It means we call it forth prophetically by faith. It is a spoken utterance that is spoken through faith and hope, knowing God's will and pressing toward that with your words.

Prophetic declaration looks more like a person prophesying from a place of faith into a specific situation. It has a powerful impact into atmospheres and present realities, calling forth a desirable change, season, or shift. It is spoken when someone understands what the Word of God says they can have, and prophesies into that to advance and move toward what they believe is God's will.

For instance, when someone feels called to be a missionary into a specific country, he or she works toward immigration visas and all the logistics of moving and finances. Often what people believe God is saying or where God is taking them is not as easy to possess or move into—it is met with levels of resistance or difficulty. And in these types of situations a prophetic declaration is spoken by a person who generates the response and speaks into the situation from a place of faith. They have a belief and hope in the outcome they believe God has promised, and thus they creatively declare into their future calling things that are not yet present.

A PROPHETIC DECREE

A prophetic decree is a definite utterance in which circumstances are directly addressed in such a way that they must immediately shift. I would compare this to a member of government, legal authority, or ruling king passing a law that immediately is brought into effect. A decree is weightier than a declaration, as it has more of a powerful faith behind it. It's the kind of faith that defies mountains and commands them to be uprooted and thrown into the sea.

A decree comes from a place of strength, because there is such an assurance and confidence in what is about to happen that the prophet is simply vocalizing a new ordinance. The main difference between the declaration and the decree is that the declaration speaks in faith from a person into a situation, whereas a decree is the verbatim word of the Lord that is conveyed from God to a person, and then the person communicates what God has declared.

These acts of decrees fulfill God's first commandment to humanity: "Be fruitful, multiply, and have dominion!" Satan constantly wants to dictate the outcome to humanity, which was a part of the curse, "And I will put enmity between you and the woman, and between your seed and her Seed; He shall bruise your head, and you shall bruise His heel" (Genesis 3:15). So the prophetic decree takes dominion back in the situations where the devil is trying to dictate your doom; instead, your decrees agree with God's blessings and promises. Besides, "We know that in all things God works for the good of those who love him, who have been called according to his purpose" (Romans 8:28 NIV).

To decree is to speak like a king who speaks and requires an initiation of change that commences as the words are spoken. It looks more like a command than a prophetic statement of faith into a specific situation. It is a demand released into the atmosphere that requires an instant response or beginning of a new season or change. This is more of a word in which God has likely expressed His exact will and word to the prophet, and with full confidence the prophet is releasing that into the earth with the full authority of the throne of God, commanding an immediate shift in a situation or circumstance. Whether or not this has an immediate response in the natural is not important; the reality is that things have undoubtedly shifted.

Daniel began a twenty-one-day fast because what he had been praying for hadn't been answered yet. At the end of the twenty-one days, an angel arrived and said:

> Do not fear, Daniel, for from the first day that you set your
> heart to understand, and to humble yourself before your
> God, your words were heard; and I have come because
> of your words. But the prince of the kingdom of Persia
> withstood me twenty-one days; and behold, Michael, one of

*the chief princes, came to help me, for I had been left alone
there with the kings of Persia. Now I have come to make
you understand what will happen to your people in the
latter days, for the vision refers to many days yet to come
(Daniel 10:12–14).*

And so we see that things will shift in the spirit realm immediately when decrees are made. It may just take time to see them shift in the natural world around us. Other times we can see immediate change right in front of our eyes.

With time and experience, however, you will learn to differentiate between these two forms of prophetic utterances. At first they may both appear similar and they may even be hard to tell apart, but the Holy Spirit will teach and train you to see the differences as you walk with Him. They are both powerful and effective life-giving words that we will use throughout our journeys, walking in this gifting and office.

CHAPTER 13

GOD DOES NOTHING UNLESS HE REVEALS IT TO THE PROPHETS

God still operates by His own principles He demonstrated in creation. The Word always precedes the Spirit and the Spirit is the one who generates the fabrication of the outworking of the Word that is declared and decreed. The Father proved this again when Jesus, who was the Word made flesh (John 1:1, 14), came before the outpouring of the Spirit in Acts 2. Throughout history, God has always needed mouthpieces on the earth, and He still needs them in our own day, to declare the word of the Lord prior to the outworking of the Spirit, delivering what was spoken. And this must happen no matter if it is a blessing, hope, and vision, or a forewarning and judgment.

God has said that He will do nothing on the earth unless He first reveals it to His servants, the prophets. Amos declared, "Surely the Lord GOD does nothing, unless He reveals His secret to His servants the prophets. A lion has roared! Who will not fear? The Lord GOD has spoken! Who can but prophesy?" (Amos 3:8)

Showing God the reverence and respect He is worthy of can only be done to its full extent inside a relationship of intimacy with Him. A prophet is not a mechanical messenger who acts like a worker on an assembly line. No. A prophet is a friend of God, an intimate confidante who is in time trained by the Lord in His ways of wisdom, understanding, and discretion.

A FRIEND OF GOD

Becoming a friend of God is and should be the primary goal of everyone's life, especially that of a prophet. The prophetic should never be an end in itself; it should always be seen as a healthy by-product that happens naturally out of relationship with Him. I value God's voice personally whispering His love for me over any great word I may hear for a church or even a nation. I prioritize my personal intimacy with Him over any form of service that I can render *for* God. Keeping this balance in my life keeps me safe.

If we look throughout the history of the Scriptures, we see case after case in which God tells people beforehand what He was about to do. God told Eve that her seed would crush the serpent's head, and He ultimately spoke of a coming salvation that came in the person of Jesus Christ. God told Noah of a coming flood and gave him instructions on how to prepare for it, so he and his family could be saved. God told Abraham He was going to destroy Sodom and

Gomorrah before it ever happened, and Abraham even prayed that God would spare them if a certain number of righteous people were found . God told Moses to declare the ten plagues He would bring on Egypt if Pharaoh failed to let Israel go. And Jesus told Peter that he would be dressed by another and led to where he did not want to go, speaking of Peter's impending death in old age by execution.

When God declares something through His prophets before it actually happens, He makes a twofold statement: God honors His word so much that He cannot break it. This is the same word that formed everything that was made in Genesis 1, with the exception of Adam, who was shaped in the hands of God and God breathed into him, thus giving him life. God has so much integrity that His Spirit can *only* respond to His word.

And so He reveals what He is about to do to His servants, the prophets. In turn, the prophets manifest the word from the spirit realm by announcing it into the natural world in which we live. They do this by not only releasing His word, but also by the actions of His Spirit. God, although omnipresent, is not yet physically standing on the earth, and so He needs the partnership of His servants to vocalize His will, warnings, and intents to the created realm. It is at that point that God has the legal right to move in the earth. His word has been sent out and He can now oversee it until it is fulfilled.

While God reveals His intents, He actually relies on prophets to release the word into the earth so that, in all things, God is found to be true. Being a prophetic son or daughter who hears God's secrets is a matter of intimacy and priorities. When this happens, you'll begin to deeply care about what God cares about, be concerned with what He is concerned with, and even experience His feelings. You begin to not just hear the voice of God as a service to Him, and to be affirmed by others as someone who hears from God; rather, you care so much for God that you genuinely and passionately care for and are even burdened for the thoughts and wishes of His heart.

In this place you are able to hear and see His secrets and the revealing of His plans. It is from that place that you are able to convey and communicate heaven's agenda, where you are not speaking the intents of a distant spiritual entity, but the words, plans, and intentions of a loving Father, who is your best friend.

One of my favorite examples in Scripture, aside from Jesus of course, is King David. He was a friend of God. In fact, God loved David's heart and there was a romance in place throughout his life with the King of heaven.

David ruled over Israel after the fall of Saul and was a good king. He was often noted as waiting on God for instructions, both before and after being crowned king. When trouble would come to him or his land, he would go and speak with his Friend, waiting for God to reveal what would happen or what he should do in each situation. Let's look at one such example.

The Philistines had aggressively come up against Israel and were moving troops into the area to invade and pillage, as they often would attempt to do. II Samuel 5:22–25 tells us:

> *Then the Philistines went up once again and deployed themselves in the Valley of Rephaim. Therefore David inquired of the LORD, and He said, "You shall not go up;*

circle around behind them, and come upon them in front
of the mulberry trees. And it shall be, when you hear the
sound of marching in the tops of the mulberry trees, then
you shall advance quickly. For then the LORD will go out
before you to strike the camp of the Philistines." And David
did so, as the LORD commanded him; and he drove back the
Philistines from Geba as far as Gezer.

Some would say this wasn't fair. God gave David the advantage; God gave him not only what to do but when to do it in order to win the battle. God revealed a secret to His servant David, and so David had the advantage over the enemy army. David, as God's close friend, had access to hear His heart. The principle is that God more often than not will reveal His secrets to those He is intimate with, rather than those who do not regard or value His heart and friendship.

MAKING GOD'S HEART OUR PRIMARY PURSUIT

Making the pursuit of God's heart primary as a son or daughter needs to be the focus of our attention and devotion. His secrets and words are secondary, which come as a result of our devotion to Him. As you grow and develop in your prophetic gift, you will begin to realize that some of what He speaks about is not for anyone else other than you—it is too intimate to share with others. And often God will test you to see if you can keep matters of intimacy a secret, and as you demonstrate this He will likely trust you with more that is in His heart.

There are discussions that take place between my wife and me in our marriage that no one will ever know about because they are private. God has much the same approach with us. He is looking for confidentiality as well as representation; primarily, however, He is looking for intimacy. So as you grow and develop in your journey of intimacy and prophetic maturing, learn to discern what God is sharing with you. Is it is for others or just between you and Him? God does nothing in the earth without first revealing it to His servants, the prophets.

CHAPTER 14

BELIEVE THE PROPHETS AND YOU WILL PROSPER

Obedience to one prophetic word has the ability to change the entire landscape of a person, a people group, a church, or even a nation. There are few people in the world whom I allow to counsel me in weighty matters on a prophetic level, and few whom I will pay great attention to when they come to me with what they claim to be the word of the Lord.

The reason I say they claim to have it is that many people will come claiming they have a word from God, but there is no substance to it, and they are either learning to discern the difference between a genuine word from the Lord and their emotions, or they are simply wanting to look gifted and anointed. I am not suggesting we become critical of and not trust anyone who wants to give us a word from God, but that we become discerning and cautious about who speaks into our lives. This goes for any area of influence.

Part of an obvious flaw in Christians at times is that the starving ones who do not know how to feed themselves and commune with the Lord, will "eat" and receive almost anything! This allows contamination and harmful words to be consumed without even looking at what it is being eaten. A healthy person, on the other hand, who is feeding him or herself on the Word, presence, and person of the Lord will have more of an understanding and level of discernment when something not quite right is presented to them. A person who is well fed will smell the spoiling milk and so reject it, whereas a person who has not had food for days or weeks may consume the bad milk without even a second thought.

We must not let a paranoia set in here, but a calm state of spirit that wisely divides the word of truth. Once we are in this position, we are well equipped to rightly weigh out prophetic words that are presented to us.

ONLY YOU ARE RESPONSIBLE

When a word from a prophet comes from heaven, and it is obvious and apparent, then we place value and importance with great attention to that word. Aside from hearing God's voice, there are probably only two people in my life whom I trust to hear God when they speak to me what God has shown them. Their consistency and track record of accuracy in hearing from God are something that are valuable in my life. But it's important that I not become dependent on these people—they bring incredible prophetic guidance and direction to my life, but I alone am responsible for the decisions of my life, doing my best to follow God's leading.

Your life is the same. Prophets and prophetic moments are like advisors in your life. But do not follow them blindly; you must take those messages and advice before the Lord and get confirmation so that you are absolutely sure that what you are hearing and being given is truly from Him. We cannot blame prophets if what they say doesn't turn out like we expected, or even if what they say is completely wrong. We have to take responsibility for the direction and decisions of our own lives.

There is one thing that is inherent in human nature, which is true all the way back to Adam and Eve: there is a radical tendency to blame others for our mistakes, situations, and bad decisions. This is why the Scriptures remind us in Philippians 2:12 to "work out our own salvation with fear and trembling."

A prophet's job is to deliver messages and keep God's people on the Jeremiah 29:11 path of God's plan. I can recall the hallmark moments in my life where I listened, and I also recall the times I did not listen to the word of the Lord from these people. Listening to God's prophets, especially those who walk closely with God, is one of the wisest decisions a person can make. In fact, it could be one of *the* wisest decisions you could make concerning your walk with the Lord.

We read in 1 Corinthians 14:31 that "all can prophesy," but then we read in 1 Corinthians 12:29 Paul's question: "Are all apostles? Are all prophets? Are all teachers? Do all work miracles?" This means not all who prophesy are prophets. No matter who it is, always weigh out each prophetic word with prayer and by seeking the face of God. Everyone can learn to operate in the gift of prophecy, but not everyone walks in the office of a prophet. There are also young prophets who are in a season of learning and developing and stepping out in their gift, and then there are those who are more seasoned, who have become more consistently accurate in their gifts.

When one of these seasoned prophets comes to me, he or she gets my full attention. They have given me forewarnings that have kept me safe from making wrong decisions, and I value their input. Only a fool would see a forewarning as a threat against his or her own person. Forewarnings are not pleasant to take at times, but if taken seriously they will keep one from walking off of a cliff. The writer of Proverbs says, "Whoever heeds life-giving correction will be at home among the wise" (Proverbs 15:31 NIV).

I have also had prophetic words of wisdom that have caused me to make right decisions, both in my personal and in my business life. It is amazing how listening to the right voice can change your life for the better. If there was someone in the secular world who could accurately predict the winning lottery numbers, he would have the ability to change someone's life in a serious way, correct? Now if that is the secular world, then how much more in the spiritual world? A prophet who really walks with God can speak of things to come and can receive messages from heaven, instructing you to sidestep danger or walk through doors of opportunity into God's blessing.

Even if you are a prophet yourself, always value and honor the prophets in your life, for the blessings they can add to your life are valuable. Certain areas in our personal lives are not always open to hearing God for ourselves, as they can be emotive areas. And so God will send someone to you from time to time. He doesn't want you going to your local prophet every second day for your "spiritual reading," much like an unsaved person would go see a tarot card reader. God doesn't want you looking to them for direction; He wants you to develop your own spiritual muscles and grow in your own capacity, to inquire of Him yourself like David did. But He also wants you to listen to His prophets when they come to you, for as you listen to them you will be blessed.

LISTENING TO THE PROPHETS

In 1 Kings 17:7–16, we read an example of blessing that comes to a widow as a result of obeying the prophet's word. There was a woman who had endured horrific loss in her life. Her husband died, so she was not provided for anymore; all of her remaining supplies had come to an end with the exception of a little oil and flour; there was no one to help her. She was destitute and alone, afraid and in the process of dying. Her situation was so bad that she had given up on even the thought of her own survival—she had settled on death.

Then in comes Elijah the prophet. Elijah confidently tells the woman to make him a small cake from the ingredients she had leftover and was about to eat before dying. It's easy to think this was arrogant and insensitive on Elijah's part, but this was a spiritual request not a natural one. We cannot assess these types of matters through our emotions. In the same way, people often become critical of tithing and giving to churches, but the criticism is because of a lack of understanding of this principle. The lady was gathering sticks for the fire that would cook ingredients for her last meal until a prophet who had heard from God came to her and told her what to do.

Elijah did not explain himself; he simply asked for a portion of her meal. She must have been upset about it. But in obedience to his word, she gave Elijah a small cake. And that moment changed her life. By obeying the instructions of the prophet, which actually came from God, she made contact with divine provision from heaven that remained constant for the rest of the famine. It's important that when a prophet has heard from God, to put our emotions, ego, and criticism aside and to carefully listen to what has been said, because a miracle could be on the way. It is amazing that both the widow and Elijah were provided for in that moment. In fact, the widow was blessed due to her obedience. Many prophets have taken advantage of this principle and hurt many people's trust. We must be careful to walk in utmost integrity around these situations.

In 2 Kings 4 we read about a certain widow whose husband had died and creditors were coming to collect her two sons to pay for the owed debt. It must have been a traumatizing situation to be in. She cried out to Elisha, asking for help, knowing the empowerment from God that the prophet carried. She explained to him that she had nothing in her house except a jar of oil. Elisha commanded the widow to borrow vessels from all of her neighbors—God was about to give her oil from heaven, and not a little.

The command given by the prophet doesn't necessarily make sense in this woman's situation. She was in extreme poverty and had no husband or income. Her two precious children were about to be taken as slaves to pay for the debt. And yet the prophet's offer of hope was to gather empty jars, and a lot of them. This is such an important lesson for us not to despise, distain, or overlook the way God can choose to bring about answers, breakthroughs, and miracles. Prophets can be so easily misunderstood in this aspect—they do not always stop to explain what is happening in the moment. They speak out what God is showing them, and if people partner with them by faith, then they will see miracles occur. Oftentimes these opportunities can be missed because people intellectualize too much, and thus they miss the whole point of what God wanted to do in that moment.

In this case, the widow did exactly what Elisha commanded. She went and gathered as many jars as she could, came into the house with her sons, closed all the doors and windows, and began pouring from the one jar of oil into all the empty jars. And a miracle happened! All of the empty jars were filled from just one jar of oil! God supernaturally multiplied the oil because she had been obedient to the word from Elisha.

She then did as the prophet had said: she sold the jars of oil, paid off her debt, and lived out the rest of her time on earth from the remaining proceeds. God is an amazing provider and miracle worker. But many times the package He delivers His blessings in is not what people expect, which is why people didn't recognize His Son when He came to the earth.

WHATEVER HE TELLS YOU, DO IT

The first public miracle Jesus did—turning water into wine—took place at a wedding in Cana (John 2). The people believed and obeyed His instructions and multiplication took place. This miracle in itself is highly prophetic and significant to the church and even the world. Of all the miracles Jesus could have done in a public way, He chose to release a creative miracle that required other people to simply believe and do what He told them to do. It was significant for many reasons.

It was a village wedding that Jesus was invited to. The family had already poured all of the wine that they had prepared for the celebration and at that point a crisis occurred—all the wine ran out! Jesus's mother, Mary, actually placed such confidence in Jesus's power that she initiated Jesus by saying to the servants, "Do everything He tells you." Jesus instructed them, they obeyed, and the equivalent of 2,100 bottles of wine were created from plain water! The servants believed the creative power on Jesus's life, and as a result they were blessed at that wedding in a notable manner—not only the servants but the entire village celebrated that day.

God has made it clear that when the prophetic is believed, honored, and obeyed, then people prosper. As prophets, it is not our job to persuade people to believe what we prophesy under the Spirit of God; however, if they do, then we will get to watch their lives be bettered for it. Prospering comes in a variety of ways—calamity can be avoided, or financial, relational, or spiritual blessing can be obtained. No matter in what area we need it, when we obey God's word coming from a prophet, we will prosper. "Believe in the LORD your God, and you shall be established; believe His prophets, and you shall prosper" (2 Chronicles 20:20).

CHAPTER 15

THE EAGLES

Most people perceive their surroundings from where they stand, but a mature prophet sees from a soaring height looking down with pinpoint accuracy. Prophets will often have a long-term perspective with a cause-and-effect awareness. They will understand that if an issue isn't addressed, confronted, healed, or empowered, then in the course of time problems could arise as a result. They will oftentimes have an acute grasp of vivid possible outcomes, and at times can seem intense as they have an insight into the chain reactions and effects that situations will present if left unchecked.

Like eagles, prophets see from a different platform. A deer, although a noble creature, has been created with a three to six-foot stature depending on breed, and it sees at ground level. A deer has a boots-on-the-ground perspective and has heightened senses to matters immediately surrounding it. An eagle, on the other hand, can soar hundreds of feet in the air and see the lion a mile away stalking the deer that is oblivious to the impending danger.

Prophets see what others don't. And when they warn people of what they see, it can seem overwhelming or intense at times, but that is because they are seeing the reality of impending threats or the proximity of impending breakthroughs, provisions, and miracles. The church needs the eagles soaring high above the ground, and then reporting back what they see.

A WATCHMAN ON THE WALL

I love the outdoors. And it is in the outdoors where we observe eagles operating in their role of hunting, specifically removing the rats and rodents and other smaller animals from their environments. That is their food source in the natural world. And farmers are thankful for this, as the rats and rodents and slightly larger animals will ruin crops if not kept under control. Eagles provide this service free of charge; it's their natural programming.

This is a picture of one of the ways a prophet will function in his or her community; a prophet will see damage or threats coming like a watchman on a wall and will look to address or confront the issue before it arises. Farmers, which can be symbolically represented in this illustration as pastors, are grateful for this function being fulfilled, as it ultimately protects the crop or the community.

Church needs to be a safe environment for everyone to come and be ministered to and receive help. But occasionally we find that people will be in church with an agenda or an unhealthy sin issue they are not looking to be freed from. They'd rather practice it, potentially affecting and hurting innocent people in the process. These people are not always obviously apparent and while we need to love everyone and not look for evil, we do need to be vigilant and aware of the evil in our midst.

To most non-prophetically inclined people, some of these insights of warning would not be obvious; however, the prophetic will see it in many cases like an eagle sees a small animal running across a field from a great height. I'm not saying that people who have sin issues are subhuman; we all have sin issues and are saved only by grace. Rather, the prophet has spiritual eyesight to see and zone in on these issues. I am not suggesting that we label people, but if they are willingly targeting the innocent or have an agenda to cause trouble, then it is a prophet's job to address this with the local church leadership and protect the innocence of those at risk, including the people themselves.

In some cases, it could be someone who is preying on congregation members financially. I have seen Satanists try to infiltrate churches that were being illuminated by the prophetic. What I am writing here is not politically correct; it is confrontational and in many cases sad and uncomfortable. But prophets have a sober responsibility to have an acute awareness of the territory around them, both naturally and spiritually. In these cases, prophets are not to throw stones; but there may be strict boundaries that need to be enforced. Also, just because prophets see things does not necessarily mean that they speak them out at that time.

I was in leadership at a local church some time ago, and I needed to give a person, who was an offender of a serious nature, three warnings with strict boundaries. If he wanted to remain a member of the church, as he claimed, then after that third time he would be asked to leave the church. Nothing was ever done of this gross sin nature, but that person was crossing lines that were willfully given and heading toward that direction. There came a point when I asked that man to leave the church, as the leadership valued the security, safety, and innocence of all our young people in the church. Many would say this is harsh and discriminating, not loving; however, we must protect the potential victims while still facilitating the opportunity for repentance, restoration, and healing in individuals with these problems. But this is not to be done at the expense of those with whom a prophet is commissioned by God to protect. That can never be defined as love.

It is sobering, yes, but an interference of that nature can disturb a child or young person's entire future. If there is a prophet not watching, then many times predators can go unchecked. These are the jobs that teachers and pastors often avoid, whereas a prophet was built for this type of confrontation. They have the eyes of the Spirit and are confrontational in nature enough to say something that needs to be said. A prophet must learn to do this in love though— an individual is never the enemy.

Maturity acknowledges that "we do not wrestle against flesh and blood," as we read in Ephesians 6:12. People are never the adversary. But people do get into agreement with the enemy by allowing strongholds into their minds and lives. Our enemy is the devil and his fallen angels in the spiritual realm, will reflect into the natural world through people who are bound. And so we must always strive to see people set free from these strongholds or the possible attack of these spirits.

In these cases, a prophet must be like an eagle, with sharp and clear eyesight, that can see into the unseen or hidden elements and motives of the heart. They will even see the secrets of people's lives, and from there they will operate in such a way that the innocent are protected. But they will also operate in a way where the bound or demonized have an opportunity to be set free as well. I didn't fully grasp this when I was younger; I saw people who were bound and operating in dangerous spirits because I saw them mainly through my emotions. We cannot do this; rather, we must allow love, the heart of God, to be the filter through which we see, move, and express these discerning insights, because God loves all people.

Something in the book of Revelation recently caught my attention. It reads:

> *Nevertheless I have a few things against you, because you allow that woman Jezebel, who calls herself a prophetess, to teach and seduce My servants to commit sexual immorality and eat things sacrificed to idols. And I gave her time to repent of her sexual immorality, and she did not repent (Revelation 2:20).*

As I read this, I realized that even God gave someone—in this case those who were seduced by Jezebel, who operated in such wickedness, time to repent. This means that God has hope for everyone in this world, victim and victimizer alike. So a prophet cannot be the judge, but only a discerner and messenger of the Judge. If God gives people time to repent, then so must we. But, lest we're mistaken, there does come a time when God will begin to deal with certain situations.

Paul also demonstrated this when a man had engaged in sexual sin with his mother. Paul advised the church to put them both out of the church and turn them over to Satan so that in the process they may be saved (1 Corinthians 5:1). It is important that we do not uphold sound doctrine without love and grace. Truth and godly wisdom are required as we administer the prophetic into and around the church body.

MOST MISUNDERSTOOD ROLE

Prophets are definitely the most unusual and misunderstood of all of the leadership roles in the church. This is often, though not always, due to the fact that they are the ones whom God uses and requires to address these hard and difficult situations. Like the eagles soaring above, flying above the fields and calmly cruising above in the winds, will suddenly swoop down and capture a rodent or a prey that it has been watching from great heights. Prophets can be like this at times, calmly observing from a distance, discerning the activities and happenings in the spirit as well as the natural.

Prophets will discern and observe many things that others will often overlook or not even notice, and then at times these prophets will enter into a situation and confront aspects that need to be addressed. At these moments people who do not understand the prophetic will often misunderstand the prophet's heart and will label and even slander them. This is why, as a prophet, you must learn to walk in the heart of God while at the same time not backing away from your responsibility as a watchman on the wall. God's invitation to all prophetic people is to walk in humility while bringing truth and confrontation at times, done in love. I'm sure many farmers are thankful for eagles and similar birds of prey flying above their crops, as they know the pest and rodents that destroy crops are going to be lunch for the eagles.

One of the reasons that prophets are not always popular is because they are prepared to do and say the things that are not always pleasant but are definitely necessary. An eagle has amazing eyesight. If you study them you will see they can pinpoint an ant moving hundreds of feet away. There is nothing they miss. They ride the wind up into a place in the sky that gives them a commanding view of all that is below. This speaks of the importance every prophet needs to place on spending time waiting on the Lord in order to rise up on eagles' wings. We need to learn to wait in His presence with a worshipful heart that climbs into the heavenly realm in intimacy, an invested life in the Word of God, a familiarity with His voice. These are the ingredients that position a prophet to see and hear like an eagle.

LOVE AND WAR

There is nothing worse than a prophet who does not recognize the prophetic even when it is blatantly obvious. An eagle's talons are powerful and can be used in both hunting and in lovemaking. A prophet is not just a warrior; he or she is a lover, too. Both love and correction must be evident in a prophet's life; they are not to be confused or overridden. But make no mistake about it, a prophet was made for war. When the eagle spots its prey, it locks its sights onto it, and then from a great height points itself downward and begins to swoop with great speed toward the prey. The prophet can at times be like a freight train dealing with what is out of place, a threat to the body or individuals or things in the demonic realm.

The prophetic aspect of the talons can be like a battering ram on city gates. For this reason, you must be absolutely sure that what you are swooping in on is in fact the truth and not a misconception. Spend much time inquiring of the Lord and getting your facts straight before you pass judgment on a matter. It's a weighty and serious thing to bring correction and confrontation to someone in the body of Christ; it shouldn't be done lightly.

Do not presume to be the local executioner at your local church. Your job should always be to love and protect God's people, and so everything you do must be through that motive. However, there are occasions in which the fallen human nature has either damaged, is damaging, or is seriously threatening the people in the local or even wider church body. When confronting, it must be done in love, but in the same breath, needs to be firmly grounded on the truth and standards of God's Word.

CHAPTER 16

THE SPIRIT AND THE WORD ARE ONE

The Spirit of God and the Word of God are partners. What does that mean? The Spirit is the very Spirit of God, and the "Word" is the Word of God, the Bible that was inspired by the Spirit. We can recognize this as the written Word of God in the Bible, but we can also see in John 1 that the Word became flesh and dwelt among us. The Word becoming flesh is, of course, referring to Jesus. So the Word can either refer to the Bible or to Jesus taking on human flesh and becoming the Word.

So when a statement is made that the Spirit and the Word are one, it's like saying that God is in perfect agreement with Himself. Even though there can be different expressions or manifestations of Himself, such as the Holy Spirit is different than Jesus, these different aspects of God's expression will never contradict each other.

For instance, the Spirit of God is never going to do anything that goes against what the Word of God outlines as spiritual laws, truths, or standards. The prophetic, which is inspired by the Spirit of God, will *never* contradict the written Word of God, the infallible Word that the Spirit has inspired. These two agree.

To accurately operate in the prophetic gift, a sharp knowledge and understanding of the Word of God is absolutely necessary! It is dangerous when prophecies start to delve into extra-biblical doctrine, or simply elevate dreams, visions, or any experience that contradicts the Word of God as more authoritative than the Bible.

It's so foolish, misleading, and perilous to preach or prophesy anything that people think they may have heard, seen, or experienced that does not line up with Scripture. John 1:1 says that "in the beginning was the Word, and the Word was with God, and the Word was God." Jesus is the Word and the Word is one with the Spirit; there are three that bear witness in heaven and these three are one.

In the simplest possible way, this means that the Word will always agree with the Spirit of God and the Spirit of God will always agree with and confirm the Word of God. There will never be any exception in this case. In Hebrews 13:8, we read that Jesus, who was the expressed representation of the Father, is the same yesterday, today, and tomorrow. He does not change, and although He may express Himself in slightly differing ways, He is consistent in His message and truth. This is why Jesus said, "If you have seen Me, you have seen the Father" (John 14:9). Let's take a look at some practical examples.

In the Ten Commandments God delivered to Moses, God commands that we should not steal. God is never going to make an exception for that in some new prophetic revelation that is given by the Spirit. Stealing is wrong, and God will never reveal through a prophet that it is okay to steal. God cannot go against His Word, for He is not a man that He should lie.

A TIGHTLY-WOVEN PARTNERSHIP

Laying the foundation of this sound belief system from the Word of God in your life will cause you to hold up a standard that will never accept or deliver a prophetic message of any kind that even in the slightest way does not agree with the Word of God. This will prevent you from being deceived. I have seen several different streams of people in the body of Christ throughout my life, and I am amazed at the high percentage of them who strongly take one aspect of God's expressed person and minimize every other aspect.

It must deeply grieve and sadden the heart of God that His Word is preached in churches but His Spirit is not welcome. On the other end of the spectrum, it must grieve Him that there are people who want to play in the river and Spirit of God with no real regard or foundation in the Word of God. Both are of these are wrong! The balance is found between these two extremes. The Word and the Spirit were designed by God as a tightly woven partnership that is to work well together. We cannot have one without the other in a healthy sense.

There is a saying that if you have only the Word, then you will dry up in religion, but if you have only the Spirit, then you will blow up in instability. But when you have the Word and the Spirit, then you will grow up into maturity.

We can see this connection between God's Word and His Spirit as the disciples engaged in the Great Commission: "And they went out and preached everywhere, the Lord working with them and confirming the word through the accompanying signs" (Mark 16:20). Signs and wonders will always follow the preaching (or teaching of the Word of God). But this also works the other way too. Signs and wonders came first on the Day of Pentecost, and when the people gathered to see what was happening, Peter preached and three thousand people were saved in a day!

It's always a mystery to me why people want to dissect the person of God! Wait a minute, we are the creation, right? We are not to dictate to God how He should be, and we have no right to limit Him to express only a part of His person. The Word is only understood correctly when it is illuminated by the person of the Holy Spirit, causing it to come to life. Likewise, the Spirit is only activated through the Word. People try to limit God to working only through one of the two but not both. But as children of God, we must pursue the fullness of God in all of His freedom.

The prophetic gift is an expression of the Spirit of God, but it must work in conjunction with the Word of God. Everything that is spoken or expressed through the prophetic gift *must* agree unwaveringly with the Word of God. If it does not line up with the Word of God, and the person prophesying claims it is a new revelation, then they are deceived at best, or deceivers at worst. The reason most people and prophets get off-track in this area is that they do not know the Word of God very well.

If you want to live safe and protected in your life, especially as you grow in your prophetic gifting, then ground your mind and spirit by reading and consuming the Word of God regularly. This will cause you to think in God's realm, it will cause your mind to function in the ways of God, so that when situations or statements are presented, your godly belief system will respond with truth that will cause you to see straight!

Become a Berean, like the apostle Paul commended in Acts 17:11. Paul commended the Bereans for being those who examined the Word of God to confirm that what was being preached and ministered by Paul was correct. Do not just believe what you hear; believe God's Word. Allow God's Word to become your benchmark, plumb line, and conscience in all matters of faith and practice.

As a prophet you need to be well versed with God's written Word so that you may serve others from a place that Paul advised his spiritual son. He said, "Be diligent to present yourself approved to God, a worker who does not need to be ashamed, rightly dividing the word of truth" (2 Timothy 2:15).

THE APPROVAL OF THE FATHER

At times various doctrines and new teachings sweep through the body of Christ. Some of these are straight from the heart of God and the Spirit of revelation, while at other times they are contrary to the Word and Spirit of God. In these instances, where they are contrary, many times the body of Christ will look to the teachers and scholars of the Word for verification, and this is where some mature prophets are crucial but often overlooked.

Prophets are the watchmen on the wall in doctrinal issues, along with the teachers. A prophet is armed with a certain hardwiring from the Spirit of God to be able to stand up and speak at certain times to confront or empower various issues. This must be done in meekness but with absolute strength and covered in the robe of humility. And because of this, a real prophet must have a soft heart and tough skin.

In the moment that John the Baptist stood up before Herod, he had this soft heart and tough skin. It is the ability to remain tenderhearted before the Spirit of God but firm and flint-faced as you go before those you are sent to, like God instructed Jeremiah in 1:4–10:

> Then the word of the LORD came to me, saying:
>
> "Before I formed you in the womb I knew you;
>
> Before you were born I sanctified you;
>
> I ordained you a prophet to the nations."
>
> Then said I:
>
> "Ah, Lord GOD!
>
> Behold, I cannot speak, for I am a youth."
>
> But the LORD said to me:
>
> "Do not say, 'I am a youth,'

For you shall go to all to whom I send you,

And whatever I command you, you shall speak.

Do not be afraid of their faces,

For I am with you to deliver you," says the LORD.

Then the LORD put forth His hand and touched my mouth,
and the LORD said to me:

"Behold, I have put My words in your mouth.

See, I have this day set you over the nations and over
the kingdoms,

To root out and to pull down,

To destroy and to throw down,

To build and to plant."

The reason that we are not to be afraid of others is that we will often stand in the office of the messenger of the voice of God to the body of Christ, which can come with great rejection and persecution. Don't just expect rejection though, because there are moments in which a prophet will deliver exciting news and empowering messages from the Lord. Those, of course, are much simpler to manage. However, when the Lord has a prophet address a more sensitive issue where the Word and Spirit are addressing a dysfunction in a particular church, then you will need to be ready to deal with people's displeasure and even reject backlashes. This is why God told Jeremiah not to be afraid of people's faces. Do not judge your success by people's approval, but rather by God's.

A prophet must have a built-in ownership of the interests of the kingdom and the approval of the Father. The ability to stand before your God and bow in humility before Him while standing boldly in the strength of the Lord before those you have been called to deliver a message to, is an art. It is formed out of walking out a process of preparation in the Spirit of God.

A prophet is without doubt called to be a watchman and the conscience to the church. As part of the fivefold apostolic team, the prophet is to monitor the purity and course, to ensure the accuracy and freedom in both the Word and the Spirit. Think of your prophetic role and office as a GPS function in the church and people's lives around you. When you take the wrong turn when driving, your GPS will announce "rerouting" and begin to recalculate the course to get your car back on track to the intended course. No one likes to hear the GPS say it is rerouting, as it interrupts what you thought you were doing. It is necessary though to get you to where you actually need to be.

There was a time years ago when a certain move was sweeping the earth and the church I was a part of started to really lean toward more of the gifts of the Spirit and began to neglect the sound teaching of the Word. Over time the Holy Spirit began talking to me about this issue, and He told me to delicately approach the pastor and bring up this problem. Very humbly I approached the pastor and addressed the issue of the lack of the Word of God being taught. The pastor did not listen to me nor receive what I had to deliver, and things continued to deteriorate until God used certain circumstances to get his attention and rectify the dysfunction of his ministry.

The point is that I was obedient and stood in my office as a prophet and delivered the message in humility as the Holy Spirit had asked me to do. Once I did that, my hands became clean and the person I delivered the message to became responsible for the word of the Lord. I continued to pray over the situation, but I had carried out the task I was given. If we fail to deliver the message that God gives to us, then we can be responsible. Just ask Jonah!

One of the most important foundational building blocks you can lay in your life and prophetic ministry is the investment of the Word of God. If you do not study the authentic and get acquainted with the nature and ways of God as revealed in Scripture, then how will you be able to decipherer between the truth and the counterfeit and not end up being misled?

The Word of God tells us, "The people who know their God shall be strong, and carry out great exploits" (Daniel 11:32). I want to encourage you to make this the hallmark of your life—that you know God, that you know His Word, and that you walk in His Spirit. As a result of this pursuit, your life and ministry will carry out amazing exploits and demonstrations of God.

Welcome to your personal school of the prophets. This is just the beginning ...

A WORD TO THE READER

It's so exciting that you have begun this journey into your destiny in the prophetic world. Always remember that God's process of developing our gifts, character, and ministries is often a longer process than we think it is going to be. Resting in His timing and allowing Him to fashion and train you in the things He has called you to is an important part of the process. Don't neglect the process for the destination—oftentimes the process is the destination. Don't try and push yourself forward; focus on today and understand that God is a God of process and time.

You are going to learn so much and grow as you walk with God and seek to grow in your prophetic gifting. This growth will come through teaching, but it will also come through mistakes. Allow all of these experiences to shape you into what God has for your life—so that you will look more and more like Jesus.

Look for the other titles coming soon in the Guild of the Prophets series. This prophetic equipping series has been designed as a school of the prophets, meant to help you grow, develop, and mature into the fullness of functioning in your calling around this amazing ministry of expressing God's heart to the world.

THE PROPHETIC TRAINING SERIES:

 THE FOUNDATIONS OF THE PROPHETIC

 THE PROCESS OF THE PROPHETIC

 THE OFFICE OF THE PROPHET

 THE EQUIPMENT OF THE PROPHET

 THE PITFALLS OF THE PROPHETIC

 THE ESSENTIALS OF THE PROPHET

 THE NEMESIS OF THE PROPHET

Order the series today and receive a discounted package price. Please follow us on Facebook and sign up for e-mail updates about upcoming books and events at www.AndrewBillings.org or www.GuildOfTheProphets.com.

Guild of the Prophets School—Coming Soon.

JOIN THE GUILD OF THE PROPHETS

Prophets need prophets; in fact, we should not isolate ourselves from others in the prophetic community. And so I want to encourage you to sign up and join the Guild of the Prophets. In joining the Guild, you will be encouraged, strengthened, and informed of additional prophetic resources, special pricing, and limited-access events that may be of interest to you. Membership is free.

You can also preorder the next book in the series and receive a discounted price. Once all seven books in the series are available, a special edition volume package price will be available to Guild members. Please follow us on Facebook and sign up for e-mail updates about upcoming books and events online at:

ANDREWBILLINGS.ORG | **GUILDOFTHEPROPHETS.COM**

Andrew Billings the author and founder of "Guild of the Prophets" was born in New Zealand.

He and his wife Rebekah now pastor their church in Orange County California – "The Dwelling Place OC."

God called Andrew as a prophet at a young age in a series of encounters and at the age of 21, Andrew had a visitation with Jesus and from that moment, the prophetic was commissioned in his life. As time went on he grew and developed as a prophet. Today Andrew has a passion to see a generation raised up with sound teaching, boldness and empowerment to walk in this calling. You can discover more at www.AndrewBillings.org.

You can also learn more in the bio section of each book in this series.

··· NEXT IN THE SERIES ···

GUILD OF THE PROPHETS

THE
PROCESS

OF THE PROPHETIC

VOL.

II

YOU WILL LEARN ABOUT:

1 — THE PROCESS OF A PROPHETIC PROMISE COMING TO PASS.

2 — UNDERSTANDING GOD'S HEART & LOVE OVER YOU.

3 — HOLDING ON TO GOD'S PROMISES THROUGHOUT YOUR JOURNEY.

4 — POSITIONING YOURSELF TO FULFILL A PROPHETIC WORD.

5 — THE REQUIREMENTS OF OBTAINING YOUR PROPHETIC PROMISE.

6 — BIRTHING GOD'S PROPHETIC PROMISES INTO REALITY.